HANN̶̶̶EY

Crazy Mama

9 Steps to a Not-So-Normal Life

www.hannahhelpme.com

CRAZY MAMA
9 Steps To A Not-So-Normal Life

Published by Team Keeley, LLC

Copyright © 2014 Team Keeley, LLC
All rights reserved. No part of this book may be reproduced in any manner whatsoever for the purposes of resale or redistribution without the written permission of the Publisher.

ISBN-13: 978-1500579463

ISBN-10: 1500579467

1st Edition
Copies of this eBook may NOT be resold or redistributed in any way without expressed and written consent by Team Keeley, LLC
www.hannahhelpme.com

ACKNOWLEDGEMENTS

Many thanks to God for giving up His only Son, so that through His suffering I am blessed, through His stripes I am healed, through his punishment I am acquitted, through His poverty I am rich, and through His brokenness I am made whole. *Phewf! That was a mouthful!* But, seriously, it doesn't make sense that Someone so perfect should take my pain; and that's just what makes it so crazy!

Thanks also go to my incredible husband who keeps believing in me, even there's absolutely no logical reason why he should. Hoooweee! I love that man o' mine! Thanks go to my seven beautiful children, who constantly amaze me with their wisdom, maturity, skill, creativity, and noise level. Thanks go to my mentors and coaches, who have poked, prodded, pulled, and prayed me along the path to greatness (you know who you are). Deepest gratitude for my fantastic editing crew—my siblings—who quickly responded to a call to proof this book over a weekend and came through for me as always. By the way, if you find an error, it's their fault.

And, a big, fat hug goes to YOU, my friend. Because of you, I get up and go to work every day. I love you and care about you more than you know. I pray for you continually and believe the best for you. You were meant to be blessed beyond belief; and I'm not going to stop until I see it happen! By the way, you're also one crazy mama!

www.hannahhelpme.com

Crazy Mama

9 Steps to a Not-So-Normal Life

Introduction

Step 1: Look Where You're Going

Step 2: Claim Your Birthright

Step 3: Live Like a Donkey

Step 4: Use Fightin' Words

Step 5: Quit Being a Cheap Copy

Step 6: Drop the Dead Weight

Step 7: Spark Your Super Powers

Step 8: Give What You Want to Get

Step 9: Follow the Blueprint

www.hannahhelpme.com

INTRODUCTION

If there's one thing that ain't working in this world, it's normal. But don't take my word for it. Look around you. Marriages are struggling, families are falling apart, and finances are a joke. If you're like me, that's not the kind of life you want. There is something in you that wants more. There's a reason you are reading these words right now; and there is a spirit within you rising up in agreement.

No, you don't want average anymore.
No, you're not content to just get by any longer.
No, you don't want to just exist anymore.

You're ready to live a life that is bigger and better than what the world offers. You're ready to have a life like the one that is promised to you in the Bible—a life that is exceedingly, abundantly beyond anything we could hope or imagine (Ephesians 3:20).

That life can happen; and it can happen to you. In fact, that's the kind of life that God wants you to live. It's bold, daring, and a bit crazy; but it's also blessed beyond measure. It's the difference between living in the pits and stepping out on stage.

I took my teenagers to a concert once and noticed that the crowd in front of the stage was becoming really packed in. People were bumping in to each other and pressing in from all sides. It was a genuine mosh pit—a stinky, sweaty, noisy mosh pit! Then, I noticed this one girl who had pushed her way to the front, reached up to the stage, and pulled herself right up there with the band. Immediately, she was standing there in the spotlight, frozen on stage and looked out at all the people in the pit below her. Then she did something that made everyone laugh and shout. She began dancing to the music! The lead singer saw her, walked over to where she was, and began dancing with her! People were amazed. You could look around the venue and see

www.hannahhelpme.com

where everyone was looking—right at the girl who had the guts to get up on stage. I can only imagine what they were thinking: 'that's one lucky girl! I sure wish I were on stage dancing.' But the truth is, she was the only one who had the guts to climb out of the pit and get on stage.

If you want to stay with normal, get used to the crowd. It's stinky, sweaty, cramped, and crowded. But, if you're ready to climb out of normal, then you've got to be willing to be a little crazy. I'm telling you, crazy works! You get what you give in life. And if you're ready to live like crazy, then God is going to bless you like crazy. You'll find yourself dancing on stage and looking out at all the "normal" people, exhilarated beyond measure and overwhelmed with gratitude that you had the guts to make the climb.

So, are you ready to get crazy?

CRAZY BONUS!
Get your FREE 2-part audio series, "Crazy Blessed!"
Just go to this link <u>RIGHT HERE</u> or visit
www.hannahhelpme.com/crazy

STEP 1
LOOK WHERE YOU'RE GOING

The summer sun beat down on our car as we headed down the rural country road. It was just me and my son, Kyler, who had just gotten his learner's permit a month earlier. I was giving him some driving tips as I drove us to the store to pick up some groceries.

"Always check in three spots before you change lanes—your side mirror, your rear view mirror, and over your shoulder," I said.

"Got it, Mom," he said.

"And remember to always keep two hands on the steering wheel, " I added.

" Mom, I think I know that," he retorted.

We continued driving down the road and I kept thinking of bits and pieces of advice I could give my son. I glanced at the side of the road and noticed that it had a pretty deep ditch beside it.

"This is important," I told him. "So listen up. Always keep your eyes on where you're going, not to either side of the road. See that ditch on the side of the road?" I asked him. Kyler looked up from his phone and glanced out the side window.

"Look how deep it is," I said, all the while looking down at the ditch on the right side of the car. "If I took my eyes off where I was going and looked at the side, I could easily veer off the road." As if on cue, the car veered off the road. I felt the car tilt as we ran into the ditch on the side of the road.

"Mom!" Kyler yelled, as he dropped his phone and grabbed the dashboard of the car with both hands.

"Shi—" I hollered, as I wrestled with the steering wheel.

Just then, we came up on a driveway and the right side of the car popped up out of the ditch and I was able to pull it back on the road again.

"—toooo," I said, my heart racing as I pulled over to the side of the road to catch my breath.

We sat there in silence, too terrified to speak a word.

Finally, Kyler pulled his grip away from the dashboard and slowly turned his head to face me. All the color had drained from his face and eyes were as big as saucers.

"Seriously?" he shouted. "You couldn't just tell me? You had to give me a demo?" He paused, took a long look out the side window, and then looked back at me. I was still clutching the steering wheel with my heart in my throat.

"And what the heck is 'shitooo?' He asked.

I couldn't believe it myself. I was an excellent driver. How in the world could I just run off the side of the road like that? And I never swear. I just don't. How could I almost let an expletive fly out of my mouth? Even if I was creative enough to turn it into "shitoo." Emergencies definitely bring out the ugly!

I thought for a while and replied, "I guess I proved my point." Then I added, "And, no, you're not allowed to go around saying, "shitoo!"

Where are You Looking?
It's one of the big rules in driving, as well as one of the big rules in life. You will go where you're looking. Wherever your eyes go, that's where you steer. It's not even a conscious thing. You just head in that direction whether you want to or not. So, the big question is this: Where are you looking?

"Where there is no vision [no redemptive revelation of God], the people perish; but he who keeps the law [of God, which includes that of man]—blessed (happy, fortunate, and enviable) is he." Proverbs 29:18

All the great successes began with a vision. Bill Gates envisioned a personal computer in every household, while everyone else was limited to thinking that computers were just bulky machines for big corporations. Howard Shultz envisioned taking something as dull and boring as coffee and turning it into something sexy and trendy. Before he came along, only old people drank coffee, and you picked it up at McDonald's for 50¢. And these visions have profited them quite handsomely.

Sara Blakely is another member of the billionaire club. She didn't like the way her backside looked in her white pants. The girdle she squeezed into left bulges in all the wrong places (as if there are any right places for bulges). So, she cut the feet off a pair of control top pantyhose and wore those under her pants instead. After taking a look at her new and improved rear view, she had the vision to bring this same transformation to women's rear-ends all over the world. Hence, "Spanx" was born. While some women were content with bumps and bulges, Sara had the vision to do something about it. And I'm grateful for her boldness every time I step in front of a camera for a full-length body shot!

If you're going to be a crazy mama who is living a crazy blessed life, it all begins with a crazy vision. Get out of your limitations, and imagine the impossible. It's okay to imagine the impossible because that's where God works best. In the words of my all-time hero, Jesus, "With man it is impossible, but with God all things are possible" (Matthew 19:26).

Too many people are dreaming little dreams, barely-get-by dreams, "just enough" dreams. They are hoping to just get through the day instead of seizing the day. They are hoping to just pay their rent instead of owning their home with no debt. They are hoping to catch the documentary on Mount Everest instead of climbing it themselves. But, God has given you big dreams for a reason. He wants you to imagine something that you could never in a million years do without His help.

If you're dreaming little dreams, you're shortchanging the God who created you. He doesn't want to do enough; He wants to do more than enough. He tells us in Ephesians 3:20 that He wants to do "exceedingly, abundantly more than we could think or imagine." If you're dreaming little dreams then that's all you'll ever have. It's the only level you'll ever reach. It's time to dream bigger. God wants to show up in your life in mighty ways. But it all begins with a vision.

Get a Crazy Vision
Before Abraham could ever accomplish the impossible, he had to get a vision for it. There sat Abraham, growing older in years and having very little to show for it. If he were living today, he would have his rocking chair pulled up near the heater, griping about all those cocky whippersnappers with their portable telephones. He was in despair because he believed his best years were behind him and he was going to end up leaving this earth with no children and no inheritance. It was a crucial time. The covenant of God lay in the balance. If Abraham couldn't be faithful, the covenant wouldn't be established. God knew the first step He had to take, the most vital step—Abraham must have a vision. He spoke to Abraham as he sat in his tent, warming himself by the fire.

"And He brought him outside [his tent into the starlight] and said, Look now toward the heavens and count the stars—if you are able to number them. Then He said to him, So shall your descendents be. And he [Abram] believed in (trusted in, relied on, remained steadfast to) the Lord and He counted it to him as righteousness (right standing with God)." Genesis 15:5,6

That's the first step: getting a crazy vision. God is asking you right now to break out of your limitations and imagine something huge for your life. And you can't do that hiding away in your tent. That's what Abraham was doing. He was hunkered down in his tent, having his own little pity party. That's when God stepped in and says, "Abraham, get your rear end up out of this tent and get out to see what MY plans are for your life."

I'm sure there have been plenty of disappointments in your life. Maybe you're feeling a bit like Abraham did on that dark night so long ago. You're staring into the fire, imagining what could have been. You're tallying up the lost dreams and the missed opportunities. You're pondering the wrong moves and the string of mistakes. I'm telling you that those voices whispering in your ear are nothing but lies! You have no idea what God wants to do with your life. But I can tell you what—it's good, and it's great, and it defies anything you could ever imagine.

That's why God had to get Abraham to get out of his limited way of thinking and get a new vision for his life. God is not limited in any way. And because you were created in His image, you don't either.

No matter how many wrong turns you've taken, He has the right turn up ahead. No matter how many disappointments, God has a new appointment for you. No matter how many losses, He's got gain in your future that will blow you away. God is not limited to your past. He's only limited by the vision you have for your future. You serve a big God, so it's time to start dreaming His way. It's time to dream big.

When my youngest daughter turned seven, her birthday was on a Sunday. And it just so happened that on that particular Sunday, the church was having a big, indoor event complete with tons of food, foam snowball fights, and huge inflatable toys. We came home from church that afternoon to enjoy some cake and ice cream and open up presents. Then, a few hours later, we all packed in to the van and headed to church for the *real* party! Kenna walked into the enormous sanctuary where all the chairs had been removed and in their place were huge inflatables—a big obstacle course with a slide and a moon bounce were sitting right smack dab in the middle. People had already begun throwing foam snowballs at each other. We walked around the corner and saw rows of tables, all of them covered with mountains of the yummiest food you would want in your belly. The entrance hall was filled with nothing but tables of desserts—cakes, cookies, cupcakes, doughnuts, strudels, fruit crisps, pies, even a big cake with the head of the Abominable Snowman coming out of the top. After a few hours of food and games, Kenna ran up to me and yelled, "This is the best day of my whole life!"

I couldn't have planned a party like that. My party was some balloons taped to the overhead light fixture in the dining room, a homemade cake, and a few presents from Walmart. There's nothing wrong with that party, but it certainly isn't extravagant.

Get this in your head: You serve an extravagant God! He doesn't do anything halfway and He certainly doesn't scrimp or cut corners. He goes over and above. The coolest thing we could imagine for our lives is nothing—*nothing*—compared to what God has planned for us. And when He does it, it's freedom. It's not us working and straining and sweating. It's just surrendering to a blessing that was there all along. It's just showing up to a party that's already going on.

For My thoughts are not your thoughts, neither are your ways My ways, says the Lord. For as the heavens are higher than the earth, so are My ways higher than your ways and My thoughts than your thoughts." Isaiah 55:8,9

Your thoughts are not His thoughts. As abundant of a life as you can imagine for yourself, God is dreaming up something better. He's miles ahead of you, so you may as well relax and trust Him to do things His way.

Sure, I could have thrown Kenna a bigger party. I could have rented out a banquet hall and gotten an inflatable or something. I could have ordered pizza and maybe thrown in an extra present or two. But, first of all, it would have been me trying to pull together the money to pay for it. And second of all, it would have been me doing all the hard work—scoping out banquet halls, sending invitations, lugging around the inflatable and blowing it up, and shopping for another present (okay, it would have been my husband, Blair, lugging around the inflatable, but you get the idea).

God is throwing a party. It's a huge party; and you're invited! It's your choice whether or not you're going to attend. God never intended for us to just get by. Too many people are living that way—just trying to make it from cradle to crypt without causing too much damage along the way. But that was never what God intended. Living a small life does not glorify an immense God. He designed you to live big, because He designed you in His image! And you can live a big life, an amazing life, a *crazy blessed life*, when you do it His way.

Get What's Coming To You

I'm so excited you're on this journey. No matter how good your life is it's going to get better. No matter how bad your life is it's going to get good. I don't know where you are in life, but I want to encourage you to stick with me and let me show you all that God wants for you.

One day I got a call from one of my lawyer friends. This was when my show was airing on public television and I was working with some sponsors. We exchanged the usual pleasantries, and then he asked me, "So, how are you profiting from your show?"

"Profiting?" I asked. "Well, to be honest, I paid myself a whopping salary of $2000 for the entire year. The rest of the money from the sponsors went straight into production costs."

"Well, how about some of the residuals? Are you getting any money from that?" He asked.

"Residu-who?" I said. "You're talking to me, remember?"

Honestly, I had no idea what he was talking about. It's amazing I could even pull a show together. Just goes to show you that when God wants something done, He'll use anyone available. I'll show you my SAT scores if you like, but trust me…God will use anyone. He's much more concerned with your availability than your capability. But, that's an entirely different subject.

"Your residual sales," He said. "According to your contract with public television, you get paid for residual sales on episodes that are run on extension."

"Okay," I told him. "I understood about five words of what you just said."

"I'll tell you what," he explained. "I have a good friend who does this for a living. If he can find any money that is owed to you according to your contract, he'll get it for you. The only catch is that he keeps 15% of any money he can find."

Well, I figured 85% of something was better than 100% of nothing, so I told him to go ahead and contact him and let's see what we can do.

About five months later, I got a sweet letter from this gentleman that had been assigned the project. Also enclosed in the envelope was a check for over $3,000! I could hardly believe it! I got more money through his efforts than I got all year long for months and months of hard work! I was shocked (in a very, very good way!).

Here's the thing—I had no idea that there was $3,000 floating out there that belonged to me. It had my name on it and was just waiting there to be claimed. It was only when my new friend began digging through the contract when we discovered what was rightfully mine. I was blessed. He was blessed. It was good all around. But if he had never taken the time to study the contract, he would have never been able to collect anything. It would have just sat there somewhere, unclaimed and gathering dust.

You have a huge inheritance with your name on it, and I want you to claim every single bit of it! You have a lot coming to you…way more than a measly $3000! But if you never take the time to dig through the contract, you'll never get what's rightfully yours. It will just sit there, gathering dust.

We're going to dig through God's Word and discover that He has a huge blessing established for anyone who is crazy enough to believe Him for it. You have got an inheritance that would blow you away. If I showed you pictures and videos and wrote it all out for you, you wouldn't even believe it. That's how huge and how crazy it is!

But that's the first step. You've got to believe it.

People often throw around the saying, "I'll believe it when I see it." That seems logical, right? You want evidence before you can claim something as yours. But that's not the way God's kingdom works. His ways are not our ways. You'll find a lot of inverse relationships when it comes to God. You get more when you give. You become first when you're last. You are exalted when you are humble. And when it comes to blessing, you have to believe it to see it.

If you want to experience this crazy life of being blessed beyond belief, you have to break out of man's wisdom, and start doing things God's way. You have to get a vision for it and believe that it *can* and *will* happen in your life. It's going to stretch your thinking and break you out of your tent. But if you want to see it happen, you've got to believe that it will.

Another Pity Party
Abraham wasn't the only one who had shake off the blues and get a vision of what God wanted to do in his life. Habakkuk was a prophet in the Bible who was at the end of his rope. Have you ever felt overwhelmed and abandoned? Then you know how Habakkuk was feeling. He was crying out to God, "O Lord, how long shall I cry for help and You will not hear? Or cry out to You of violence and You will not save?" (Habakkuk 1:2). That's when God spoke up. And, boy, did He—

> "Look around [you, Habakkuk, replied the Lord] among the nations and see! And be astonished! Astounded! For I am putting into effect a work in your days [such] that you would not believe it if it were told you." Habakkuk 1:5

The Lord was doing the same thing for Habakkuk that He was doing for Abraham that night. Habakkuk also had a pity party going on. The reason God seemed far away is because He was, at least in His way of thinking. Again, God's ways are nothing like ours. And the more you discover His character, the more you can rest in His way of doing things and just enjoy the party. But partying was the last thing Habakkuk had on his mind.

Habakkuk was thinking small. He was just seeking help for himself. He felt overwhelmed by the circumstances. He found himself in a mess and was crying out for deliverance. But, God was thinking bigger. In essence, He was telling him, "Quit yer bellyachin'! Look around and see what I'm up to! It's huge! It's astonishing! It's so big you wouldn't believe it if I told you." God doesn't want us to live in desperation when we could live in divinity.

So often, we become so consumed with our circumstances that we can't see that God is up to something big. We become like Habakkuk, wringing our hands and looking around us at everything that is not going right. We feel abandoned, overwhelmed, and fretting over the future. But first we have to get past ourselves. And that can be the hardest part. But here's the great news. God is leading you somewhere to bring you blessing, so your joy can be full and complete. We always have to go through the toughest climb to get to the highest peak.

The enemy certainly doesn't want you to live an abundant life, so he's going to put every obstacle in your path. But when God gives you a dream, no power on heaven, earth, or under the earth can stop you from reaching it. The only thing that can stand in the way is you. Keep that vision alive! The unknown can be scary, but God is already there. And the more you know God, the less you fear the unknown.

Ready to Think Big?
You've got to see where you're going. Quit looking around at your current limitations and develop an unlimited vision of something bigger and bolder. You've got to see it so clearly that it becomes your new reality. You know you're thinking big when your vision of where you are headed becomes so real to you, it is as if it has already occurred.

Crazy Mama

When I was a little girl, I decided I was going to build a storm shelter for my family (pretty darn thoughtful of me, huh?). So, I got a shovel and started digging in what I deemed as the ideal location. Right behind the grapevines, next to the tool shed, on our *neighbor's property!* After I got about a foot into the hole, I realized it was going to be too much work than I had intended, so I enlisted the help of a few neighborhood friends. As payment, I promised them that they could use the shelter in the event of a life-threatening emergency (even more thoughtful of me).

While they dug away, I drew up the plans. It would have two bedrooms, a dining area, a bathroom, and a reading nook. Pretty soon, word spread that Hannah was busy with another one of her projects. The neighbors wondered how long this little adventure would last. Our next-door neighbor wondered when it was finally going to be safe to fill up the hole with dirt. But I didn't see a hole in the ground. I saw something much bigger—a top-of-the-line storm shelter, complete with amenities. This vision was enough to keep me digging away toward my dreams. I never did carve out my storm shelter, but I got probably as close as any nine-year-old girl ever has.

Think big and see it clearly. Focus on the life that you are headed toward. Think about that storm shelter. Keep your vision right in front of you. But understand that just like Abraham and Habakkuk, it's not always going to come easy. There will be times of testing, so see what you're made of; and sometimes, the effort becomes way more than you anticipated. It would have been easy at any point to drop my shovel and go back to playing with my dolls. But the easy road is never going to lead you to an abundant life. That's when you need to call in some help. Surround yourself with people who make you a better person. You don't need anyone who's going to pull you down or dismiss your dreams. You need people who will grab their shovels and help you dig, people who see the big picture and believe in you.

Along with a support system, you need to keep a crystal-clear vision in front of you. My storm shelter plans even had a reading nook. Think details! You've got to be able to imagine it clearly and distinctly, even if your life circumstances seem to be taunting you, telling you it will never happen, not in this lifetime. You must see it. Until you can see the big picture, you will never be able to live it.

And more than anything, you've got to believe it is possible. Of course, I heard what the neighbors were saying. "A little girl can't build a storm shelter!" They would step out on their front porches, shake their heads, and just laugh at this girl's silly antics. When you start to dream big, there will be people left and right trying to shoot those dreams back down to reality. Don't listen! Nothing—*nothing*—is impossible with God. Scripture says, "Greater is He that is in you than he that is in the world." The world will tell us—in no uncertain terms—what is possible and what is impossible. It's time to break free of that thinking because what you have inside of you is greater than anything that the world could threaten us with. Your thinking needs to line up with a new reality, a reality where all things are possible. There are no limits for you, aside from the ones you set for yourself. Quit looking at where you are and start focusing on where you're headed.

Thinking bigger than your current situation also means thinking bigger than your circumstances. But I hear you. You may be saying, "Hannah, you don't understand what I'm dealing with. It's just too much." Maybe your kids seem to fight constantly. Maybe you can't pull together enough money to get five gallons of gas. Maybe your spouse always seems to be criticizing you. Now is when you need to think big and expand your vision. It's more important than ever that you think outside of your circumstances. Life will always throw things at you that can knock you flat. But you are bigger than that! If the spirit of the Living God resides in you, then nothing—nothing—can take you under. You are more than a conqueror through Jesus Christ! You don't have anything to fear. Fear should be scared of YOU!

You know deep down inside that you were meant for something bigger. Stop hiding from it and start believing for it! There's a huge party going on and you're invited. Are you going to come up with some lame excuse to stay home? Step out of your comfort zone because the only thing comfortable about it is that you don't have to face any fears, take any risks, or live with disappointment. But guess what, that's life. You're only going to get out of it what you put into it.

Meant to be Blessed

His goal is to bless you. He designed you to be blessed. He had abundance and joy in store for you since the beginning of time and has been moving heaven and earth on your behalf. It's time for you to see what He's up to and step into the life He wants you to live. Because the harsh truth is that even though God has immense blessing set apart for you, He won't and can't get it to you unless you're ready and willing to receive it.

Today is your day. Today is when you pull away from that little fire you slaved over and step out of your tent to view the stars. Today is when you look beyond yourself and get a vision for this crazy blessing God is up to. Right now it's bigger than you can imagine. It's too huge to comprehend. But it can be yours.

Stick with me on this journey. You're going to find things out that are going to rock your world and shake your foundation. I remember when my eyes were first opened to the blessing God had in store for me (and all those who are crazy enough to believe Him). I would lie in bed, reading the Bible, and getting chills all over at what the Holy Spirit was revealing to me.

'Could this really be true?' I thought to myself. 'Is this blessing for me?'

I grew up in the church. I became a Christian when I was nine years old. When I was ten, I baptized my cat, Fat Max, in my uncle's electric water fountain lawn fixture. So, you can see I've been pretty serious about my faith ever since I was a child! I thought I knew everything there was to know about it. Jesus died for my sins. I was going to heaven. 'Nuff said, right? Wrong!

Blessing is something that the church doesn't often teach about. It's like it's almost too good to be true. Why get anyone's hopes up? What if it doesn't work out? But I'm asking you, "What if it does?" God's word says it will; and that's why I'm putting all my chips in His corner (and pray that He has mercy on me for using a gambling reference).

When I first studied blessing, I wondered why I had never been taught this before. Then I realized that Satan has kept us deceived and in the dark for a reason. If we knew how much blessing is entitled to us through Jesus Christ, then we may act on it. And if we act on it, then we would become dangerous to the enemy and his kingdom.

Well, it's time to get dangerous!

Just like my lawyer friend who dug through my contract to find every penny that was meant for me, we're going to roll up our sleeves, dig through the Word of God and claim every bit of blessing that God has set apart for you. We'll stretch reality a bit and pretend that I'm your "lawyer." Just, please—*please*—don't ask me to wear a dark blue business suit. I may break out in a rash. But you better get dressed in something, because we're going on a journey. You've got the vision now. You know where you're going. And I'm not going to quit until you get there. You can quit if you want. But I'm not going to quit on you.

I want you to be blessed!

God wants you to be blessed!

Now it's in your corner. Aren't you sick of mediocrity? Aren't you tired of just getting by? Do you feel like Abraham, mourning over days gone by, or Habakkuk, freaking out over the days that lie ahead. Well, now is your time, and right here is the place. Do you believe it? Can you see it?

I declare with everything in me that a new vision is rising up within you. Right now, under the authority of Almighty God and in the name of Jesus Christ, supernatural ideas are springing forth in your spirit. New dreams are being birthed and old dreams are being resurrected from the dead. Your vision is being painted in perfect clarity in your mind; and your imagination is bursting forth with creativity. Your crazy blessed life is beginning now.

CRAZY BONUS!
Did you download your FREE "Crazy Creed" poster?
Print it out and post it somewhere you will see everyday!
Click on the link <u>RIGHT HERE</u> or visit
www.hannahhelpmc.com/crazy

www.hannahhelpme.com

STEP 2
CLAIM YOUR BIRTHRIGHT

Karis threw open the front door, and, being the typical teenager, tossed his backpack on the floor, collapsed on the sofa, closed his eyes, and placed his hand on his belly.

"Mom, I am *so hungry!* I need food—*now!*" he moaned.

"Well, hello to you, too," I said.

"Sorry," he replied. "I'm just starving."

I've always found it amazing how many times my teenagers can be "starving" in one day. They wake up starving. They get out of school starving. They're starving before they go to bed. One time, Karis ate eleven hot dogs at one of our cookouts. No kidding—eleven hot dogs. Two hours later, he was starving.

"Why are you so hungry?" I asked. "Didn't you eat lunch?"

"No," he answered. "I forgot to bring a lunch."

"Karis!" I said. "I even reminded you before you left the house to pack a lunch! Why didn't you do it?" Have you ever wondered why we ask our kids, "why?" so many times? When it's almost invariably followed with, "I don't know."

"I don't know," he answered. Yeah, didn't see that one coming.

"Then why didn't you just buy a lunch?" I asked him. He sat up on the sofa and looked at me.

"What would I buy it with—my good looks?" He said. I have to admit it. The boy is pretty darn good-looking. However, his looks certainly weren't going to get him a slice of pizza at the school cafeteria.

"I put $20 on your cafeteria account the other day," I said. "You had plenty of money to buy some food." He got this pained expression on his face and gripped his stomach harder.

"I could have bought some food? Aaargh!" he yelled.

(But he didn't sound like a pirate. He sounded more like a teenage boy who had officially entered the final stages of starvation. "Aaargh" was the closest I could come to writing it out in text. Just use your imagination.)

"Can you drive me back to school and let me get some pizza?" He asked.

"I don't think you'll make it," I said. "You may pass out before we get there. But don't worry. I'm on it." I opened the fridge and looked inside.

"Here you go," I told him. "Here's some leftover vegetable soup and some cold cornbread from dinner last night."

"Aaargh!" he yelled.

You are Blessed!
There's no doubt about it. People are starving today. There's nothing worse than hunger. It's gnawing pain is relentless and all you can think about is food. I remember the first time I tried to fast for thirty days. I made it three. All I could think about was food. I saw food. I smelled food. I dreamed of food. I remember lying in bed dreaming of chocolate chip pancakes and waking up to find my hand gripping an imaginary fork and my mouth wide open. Yeah, it was that bad!

But even worse than physical hunger, is spiritual hunger. People are spiritually starving to death every single day of their lives. They go through life wondering why they feel so desperate and anxious. They wake up with fear. They go to bed with worry. They dream of freedom and relief, but their reality is bondage. And the saddest thing about it is, the food is right there for the taking. It's all found in the Word of God. They have a blessing, but are not accessing it. Just like Karis and the credit on his cafeteria account, the money was there, but he didn't realize it. As a result, he was going hungry.

There is a blessing on your life. It's a huge blessing and it's right there for the taking. You don't have to live in bondage. You don't have to "deal" with life. You have the authority to call the shots. But what you don't know can leave you starving. And here's the truth: People have no idea how much blessing is available to them right now. When you are born into the kingdom of God by accepting Jesus as your Savior, you have an incredible inheritance—a birthright—that's coming to you. Question is, are you going to claim it?

A Quick History Lesson
When God created the world, it was just a natural extension of His glory. God is expansive. You just can't contain that much love and abundance. And we are just an extension of Him. He even explained in Genesis that He made man in His image. That means all the power, glory, and creative energy that belongs to God also belongs to us. How incredible is that? His intent was for us to "be fruitful and multiply." That doesn't mean that we were just supposed to have a bunch of kids (although it seems like Blair and I are taking that pretty literally). What that means is, we are supposed to expand, just like God. We are supposed to be productive and multiply our resources. It was a covenant blessing between God and His creation.

But then we had to go and mess the whole thing up. Remember the tree of the knowledge of good and evil? It was planted in the Garden of Eden and God was very specific about what they were supposed to do with it. God told them that they were supposed to care for the whole garden but they were not supposed to eat from that tree. Let me clarify that, just in case you missed it. We are supposed to care for everything God gives us authority over, but what belongs to God needs to go back to God. I believe His plan was for them to offer up that fruit to God, as a way of showing gratitude. But, Eve and Adam decided to take a bite. We could say they were tricked, but that's just an excuse. They had a choice, and made a bad one (just like many of us). God's blessing is such a powerful force that Satan would do anything to get at it. It makes him mad as hell that we are entitled to that blessing and authority and not him.

Just a little side-note that I've got to throw in this history lesson: If you want to be blessed like crazy, you've got to make sure you are giving God what rightly belongs to Him. Are you giving him the first fruits of your time? Your money? Your energy? I see people going bankrupt for their lack of discipline in tithing. Or people stressed out at work and not able to take a day of rest. God's design is perfect. When we go messing with it, just like Adam and Eve did, it's always going to come back and bite us in the butt.

And it definitely bit Adam and Eve in the butt. Satan didn't trick them. He was just crafty enough to know which buttons to push to get them to sin and fall out of the blessing. He always uses the same tricks. The reason he does is because we always seem to fall for them! He said the exact words that man always wants to hear, "You will be like God" (Genesis 3:5). Isn't that what always gets us into trouble? When we try to take matters into our own hands and do things our way instead of God's way? The truth of the situation was that they were already like God. Satan was just trying to make them think they were missing out. Well, they were missing out. They were missing out on disease, destruction, depression, pain, separation, and all the other things that God never wanted for His children. They took what was God's and made it their own; and life was never the same again.

After that bite, the knowledge of good and evil began to be played out in their lives. Up to that point, their lives were only good. They didn't have any knowledge of a difference between good and evil, because evil could not get close to them. It wasn't allowed to touch them because they lived under the protective blessing of God. It was all good. But not anymore.

From that point on, God was on a mission to restore that original blessing. He kept it alive through a handful of righteous people who decided to fight the odds and live with integrity. He found Noah and used him in a mighty way to keep his covenant blessing alive. When the earth dried out and Noah and his family stepped out of the ark, God's commandment was the same, "Be fruitful and multiply."

He kept His covenant blessing alive through Abraham, who was willing to live by faith and not by sight. When Abraham was dedicated enough to not even hold back his only son, God promised him that he would also be fruitful and multiply. He promised him abundance in every area of his life and that no evil could touch him. God's will was the same then as it is for us now—that we expand and multiply as we walk in His covenant blessing.

There was Joseph, who went from a prison to a palace in one day. There was Ruth, whose dedication took her from begging for food in the fields to owning the fields. There was David, who went from caring for sheep to caring for a kingdom. God's covenant blessing was on all of these people, and many other great men and women of faith, to expand their influence and multiply their resources. And they were all in the same bloodline. This covenant blessing that was breathed into Adam, ran through his bloodline, and into his descendants. Generation after generation of this blessing, all leading up to the birth of Jesus Christ.

He was the One. He was the Son of God, although He always referred to Himself as the Son of man. He was Lord of everything, although He insisted on being a servant. He knew no sin, but in His love, He became sin for us. A glorious exchange happened when Jesus died on the cross. He took our punishment so we could share in His glory. He took our pain and gave us His righteousness.

What does this mean for us? It means that when we make Him Lord of our lives and believe that He died for our sins, we are now part of His family! We are in that covenant bloodline of blessing! Just like a branch is grafted into a tree, or a shoot is grafted into a vine, we are grafted into the family of God through the sacrifice of Jesus Christ. His blood now runs through us and we are heirs of His abundance. Paul explained it to the people in Ephesus like this:

"But God—so rich is He in His mercy! Because of and in order to satisfy the great and wonderful and intense love with which He loved us, even when we were dead (slain) by [our own] shortcomings and trespasses, He made us alive together in fellowship and in union with Christ; [He gave us the very life of Christ Himself, the same new life with which He quickened Him, for] it is by grace (His favor and mercy which you did not deserve) that you are saved (delivered from judgment and made partakers of Christ's salvation). And He raised us up together with Him and made us sit down together [giving us joint seating with Him] in the heavenly sphere [by virtue of our being] in Christ Jesus (the Messiah, the Anointed One). He did this that He might clearly demonstrate through the ages to come the immeasurable (limitless, surpassing) riches of His free grace (His unmerited favor) in [His] kindness and goodness of heart towards us in Christ Jesus." Ephesians 2:4-7

That's so God! In His mercy, He provides a way to bring us back into that original covenant blessing. We didn't deserve it, but He did it anyway. His own son died so that we could live. He was wounded so we could be healed. He was made impoverished so we could experience abundance. He raised us up and planted us right there, by His side, where His heir sits. And check out why He did it—to show the limitless, surpassing riches of His free grace! Grace is another way to say, "undeserved favor." No, we don't deserve the crazy blessing that comes along with being in the covenant of God and that's what makes it so incredibly amazing.

The same blessing and favor that was originally breathed into man is now ours. We are to be fruitful and multiply. We are to live expansive lives of growth and abundance. So, here's the kicker! If this blessing belongs to us, if we are heirs of God's glory, if it's true that we are given limitless, immeasurable riches, then why do our lives sometimes....*stink?*

The Keys to the Kingdom

We have a lot of traditions in our family, and one of them is that we always go to the pool the first day of summer. It's our official, "School's Out!" celebration. One year, I arrived at the pool with a van full of excited kids. We piled out with our floaties, sunblock, and water bottles, and ran to the front gate. Just a couple weeks before, I had paid our registration fee and received our pool key. The kids were jumping up and down, eager to be the first people in the pool. One of the advantages of homeschooling your kids is that you can declare summer a couple weeks early and enjoy the neighborhood pool all to yourselves!

There wasn't another soul there! I was putting my key into the padlock that latched the gate shut when something totally unexpected happened. My key wouldn't fit. I checked it and double-checked it. I tried it over and over. Finally, I decided to go radical and jump the fence! I figured it wasn't trespassing because I already registered (or maybe that's just how I validated it at the time).

Very carefully, I managed to get halfway up the chain link fence in a swimsuit without losing too much dignity. However, whipping my leg around and straddling the top of the fence was an entirely different issue. I got one dimpled thigh over the top just as I heard the sound of a truck pulling into the parking lot. I was faced with a decision—stay perched on top of the fence while my kids congregated around me, or swing my other leg around and make a jump for it. I prayed that my modest swimsuit would stay modest and chose the later. Now, I was awkwardly standing inside the pool gate while my kids were on the other side of the fence, staring back at me. It was obvious I hadn't thought this one through.

The truck parked and a large man got out and made his way to the pool, laughing the entire time. I guess my antics had not gone unnoticed! He walked up to the gate, stood with my kids, and looked back at me through the fence

Yeah, it was bit awkward.

"I think you might need a key," he said, trying hard to control his laughter.

"I do have a key," I said. "It just didn't work." I was silently praying that he wouldn't kidnap my kids and leave me stuck inside the fence. Then slowly pulled out his key and slipped it effortlessly in the lock. As the lock fell open, he just smiled at me.

"Kind of like that?" He asked.

"Yeah," I answered. "Kind of like that!"

As embarrassing as that experience was for me, it taught me one very important thing. Okay, two. It taught me that modest swimsuits are a gift from God; and that if you want to reach the true treasure in life, you have to have the right key (not a defective one).

So many people are trying to get prosperity, peace, health, and abundance; but they are using defective keys. They work their tails off or sacrifice everything. They scrape and claw, or spend endless hours wising and dreaming. None of that works. It just leaves you feeling desperate.

The truth is you are blessed, but you will never be able to activate that blessing in your life unless you use the right keys.

The First Key: Know Who You Are
You are a child of the Most High God. All authority on earth has been given to you. But, you have to see yourself the way God sees you. You can't be blessed in life if you still see yourself as defective, unskilled, or lacking. What is God's is now yours. God sees the potential that lies inside of you, but you will never be able to release that potential until you can get into agreement with Him.

Gideon is a perfect example of someone who didn't have a clue as to what lay inside of him. Many people just know Gideon as that guy who passes around Bibles at hotels, but the story goes a little deeper than that. Gideon was "just a guy." Have you ever fallen into that trap? Thinking you are "just a (fill in the blank)?" For so long I thought I was, "just a mom." What does that mean anyway? I've never met a surgeon who says, "I'm just a surgeon" or an attorney who says, "I'm just an attorney." Where do we come across saying anything derogatory about the role God has given us?

But, that's the trap we fall into. God's ways are not the world's ways. If we begin to measure our worth according to the world's standards, we will always fall short. But if we can see ourselves according to God's standards, our entire perspective changes. Gideon was in that trap. He was seeing himself according to the world's standards.

First let me give you a little back-story. Gideon was an Israelite, but the neighboring countries would constantly raid their land and take everything they worked for. They wasted the land as they entered it. I guess you could liken that to kids coming home after school to a clean house and trashing it. Check it out:

"For whenever Israel had sown their seed, the Midianites and the Amalekites and the people of the east came up against them. They would encamp against them and destroy the crops as far as Gaza and leave no nourishment for Israel, and no ox or sheep or donkey. For they came up with their cattle and their tents, and they came like locusts for multitude; both they and their camels could not be counted. So they wasted the land as they entered it." Judges 6:3-5

Have you ever felt like that? Like you work your hiney off and never see results? You plant seed and never see the fruit? As soon as you do something worthwhile, along come forces you can't control and obliterate it. If you've ever organized a toy cabinet and then let kids loose in the room, then you know what I'm talking about. Or the teeth-grinding scenario when you wash and fold clothes and then see them scattered on the floor, or worse, tossed back into the laundry. Sometimes we feel like we're just spinning our wheels and all our efforts seem to add up to nothing.

The Israelites felt this same way. They would grow crops only to have them destroyed by their neighbors. And the forces were too big to overcome, so big that they "could not be counted." Every effort was just wasted. I'm sure you can imagine how Gideon felt, an Israelite just trying to scrape by and make it through the day. But who could ever imagine what would happen next?

Gideon was sitting outside, trying to beat wheat in a winepress. Sounds ridiculous, right? You beat wheat on a milling stone, not in a winepress. But he was doing that in order to try to hide it from the Midians. He knew that as soon as the Midians found the wheat, they would steal it from him. If you've ever bought some devil's food cookies and stashed them behind the vitamins to hide them from the kids, then you understand Gideon's motive here.

So an Angel of the Lord walked up to him and said, "Yo! Gideon! The Lord is with you, you mighty man of valor!

Gideon replies, "Dude! If the Lord is with me, then why is my life so rotten?"

Okay, maybe the conversation didn't go exactly like that, but the point is God saw something in Gideon that he did not see in himself. God loves to mess with us, because He knows that's the only way to pull out the magnificence He placed within us. We never really know our abilities until we are faced with the extreme. And God is extreme! There you are, stuck in the muck of daily life and just trying to make it from dawn to dusk. Then God steps in, pulls us up, shakes us off, and sticks you right in front of his Holy mirror. He called Gideon a "mighty man of valor." According to Merriam-Webster, valor is the strength of mind or spirit that enables a person to encounter danger with firmness. Did you know that you are a mighty person of valor? There is strength of mind and spirit within you that you don't even know exists. God placed greatness in you before you were even born. You have the DNA of God Almighty inside of you!

According to I Corinthians 2:16, you have the mind of Christ. According to II Corinthians 5:21, you are the righteousness of God. Isn't that amazing? When you make Jesus the Lord of your life, you take on all of His qualities in your life. His mind becomes your mind. His righteousness becomes your righteousness. His attitude becomes your attitude.

"Say Whoodat?" you may be asking yourself. "If my mind is supposed to be like Jesus' mind, then why do I want to beat my kids with a frying pan and break a beer bottle over my husband's head?" Easy! You're human. God knows this and, fortunately, His mercy endures forever. You can never be so rotten that you separate yourself from the love of God (and believe me, I've tried). God is always teaching you who you are. And the more willing of a student you are, the more like Jesus you become.

Understand that those qualities are already there. But all things start out as seed. Peace, patience, kindness, goodness, and all those other fruits of a Spirit-filled life are already within you, they are just in seed form at the beginning (one reason they're called fruits). You grow them in your life by watering them with prayer and feeding them the Word of God, and eventually, they start growing in your life. It's kind of like running a marathon. All the muscles that I need to run a marathon are already in my legs. It just takes training—and lots of it.

But training can be difficult. And when we just start out, we are likely to trip, fall, and fail miserably. Has this ever happened to you? God gives you a big dream for your life and begins to show you who He created you to be. And there you sit in your filthy kitchen with a pile of past due bills on the counter, gripping your frying pan and thinking, "Seriously? I am meant to prosper in everything? I'm supposed to be living an abundant life? His plans for me are good, pleasing, and perfect? Well, I'm just not seeing it." That's right where Gideon was. God had the audacity to call him a "mighty man of valor" and Gideon responded by expounding on his miserable life.

God wants you to think outside of your circumstances. Until you can develop a vision for who God created you to be, you will remain right where we are. God is not limited by your circumstances. The only thing that limits God's work in your life is your belief. The biggest challenge you will probably ever have in your life is believing God is who He says He is and will do what He says He will do. This is faith. Faith looks beyond where you are and focuses on where you're going. God has something incredible to do with your life, but you will only get there when you get crazy enough to step out and believe it.

The Second Key: Know What You Do
You can know who you are, but if you don't know how to act on it, you'll never get to your crazy blessing. When God begins to reveal to us who He created us to be, our first battle is with God—if we can trust Him or not. Then our second battle is with ourselves—if we can do what He tells us to do. God told Abraham He was going to bless him like crazy, that everything he did would prosper and nothing evil could ever touch him, with one very important condition. It's the word, "IF." God said, "IF you will obey me. IF you will worship only me. IF you will follow my commands." We want the blessing of God, but we don't always want to do what we've got to do to get it.

God can't bless us with financial abundance if we fail to follow His commands on how to manage the money He's already given us. God can't bless us with a healthy life if we fail to follow His commands on how to take care of our bodies. God can't bless us with fulfilling relationships if we fail to follow His command on how to treat people with honor and respect. Many people look at the Ten Commandments and see them as Ten Confinements. They believe they are God's list of "Thou Shall Nots" that He created in order to spoil all our fun. Actually, it's just the opposite. God didn't lay out His commands to limit us. He laid out His commands to expand us!

If you've ever tried to live a life out of God's commands, you know it is complicated, destructive, and stressful. Sex outside of marriage is complicated. Letting greed direct your financial decisions is destructive. Working seven days a week is stressful. God wants us to live a life of freedom and abundance and that can only happen when we follow that two-letter word, IF.

God gave us His commands to show us how loving and generous He really is. When He tells us not to worship other gods, He is saying, "You don't need any help from any other source. I am everything you will ever need and will provide for you every step of the way." When He tells us not to covet someone else's belongings, He is saying, "You don't need to envy other people. Follow my directions and I will make *you* the envy of others!"

Do you see it? Do you see how important and vital those keys are? First you have to get into agreement with God about who you really are. Then you have to get into agreement with God about what He has called you to do. It's not always easy, but it will always, *always* be worth it! And the great news is that God will never expect you to do something that He won't give you the power to do.

God told Gideon to go defeat the Midianites, which were too numerous to even be counted. There was no way Gideon could have done that in his own power; and God never expected him to. God never looks for people who are capable. He looks for people who are available and obedient. When you become available to God and are willing to obey Him, be ready to do the impossible.

God doesn't give us an easy road. If He did, we could travel down it in our own strength. God leads us to a mountain that is too big to climb without His help. This is so we can experience the freedom and joy of letting God's strength pour through our weakness. You may feel like you're facing an impossible situation right now. And, sometimes, when God takes a hold, what he asks you to do about the situation seems even more impossible. As usual, God defies logic.

One of my dear friends struggled for years in her marriage, always looking for either a way to change her husband or a way to leave him. When I would mention his name, she would make a gagging sound like she was going to puke. Yeah, it was *that* bad! Then God revealed to her what He wanted her to do—stay in the marriage, humble herself, and look for ways to bless her husband. To her, this seemed impossible. She could hardly stand to be in the same room with her husband, much less look for ways to bless him. Instead of picking up his shoes and putting them in the closet, she wanted to chuck them at his face. He wasn't abusive in any way. She just hated the thought of being stuck with him. However, when she stepped out in obedience to God to do the impossible, she found God's strength and love pouring through her. It wasn't right away. In fact, it took years. But her obedience paid off. Her husband actually became more lovable to her and she found herself enjoying the time they spent together. Now, they're stuck together like glue. Their marriage seemed impossible until she let God take hold of it.

Please listen to me—God will always ask you to do the impossible because He wants to be God. He doesn't just want to be a crutch you use when times get tough. He wants to be your total and complete power source. The impossible is nothing when it comes to God. He does the impossible every single day! When we're plugged in to this power source, we can do the impossible, too.

Puny God!
You may feel like Gideon when God asks you to do the impossible—totally and completely incapable. Good! That's right where God wants you. If you thought you could do it on your own then guess who would get the credit—you! God won't share the stage with anyone. If you want to do something great with your life, it's going to have to be God doing it through you because you're too puny.

One of my favorite scenes in the movie "The Avengers" is when Loki starts going on and on about being a god. The Hulk, tiring of the pompous drivel, grabs Loki's ankle and just tosses him back and forth on the ground, creating huge divots in the concrete and beating Loki within an inch of his immortal life. As Loki is lying there in a heap of crumbled concrete trying to recover, the Hulk walks away and dusts himself off, saying, "puny god!"

That's what we are—puny gods. We will always struggle with wanting to control our own lives and getting our own way. But when we do that, we are trying to play God's role. Until we can humble ourselves to obey God and follow His direction, we will always come up short. We're puny gods. We can try to run our lives, but we can't see past right now. God sees for eternity. We run out of steam. God endures forever. We're human. He's God.

Know who you are. You are God's pride and joy. You are made in His image. You can do all things. Not some things—all things. But here's the trick: You can do all things through Christ Who strengthens you. No one can mess with you. You plus God are a majority. Just remember to stay on the right side.

One of the coolest things about the exchange between the Angel and Gideon is that even after Gideon said that he was the poorest and puniest man in his entire clan, the Angel didn't say one word in opposition. He didn't give him the old, "chin up, chap. You can do it!" speech. He didn't need to. He simply said, "God will be with you." Where God directs you, He protects you. Where He guides, He provides. Sure, they sound like really good sayings to stick on your fridge, but they become something totally different when you apply them to your life. If God has given you a vision for your life, He is more than enough to bring it to pass. First you have to realize who you are and then you have to trust Him enough to let Him have His way.

I declare right now that you are mighty. You are full of valor. You have the strength of God within you and the peace of Jesus Christ pouring through you. You were created to do the impossible; and no force can ever prevail against you. You were designed to succeed and prosper, even in adversity. You are not subject to your circumstances. Your circumstances are subject to your God. Know this. Believe this. You are everything God says you are and you can do whatever He says you can do.

CRAZY BONUS!
Check out the FREE video, "Birthright!"
Click on the link RIGHT HERE, or visit
www.hannahkeeley.com/blog/birthright
BTW...
If you're enjoying this book,
please post a review at hannahhelpme.com/crazy.

STEP 3
LIVE LIKE A DONKEY

I glanced into the rearview mirror as I backed out of the driveway and saw my ghastly reflection—two black eyes and a swollen, broken nose. I don't know why people call black eyes, "shiners." There was nothing shiny or pretty about those things—even after I piled on a ton of concealer and dusted powder over them. I just looked like a woman with black eyes who was trying desperately to *not* look like a woman with black eyes. I wanted to hunker down at home and ride it out, but everyone knows that home is usually the last place you can find a stay-at-home mom. I had to drop the older kids off at school and take the younger ones to story time at the bookstore; and I was positive that people were either going to think my husband was doing a number on me or I had just had a nose job. Given the fact that we drove around in a rickety old 15-passenger van and I toted around a backpack instead of a Chanel bag, I didn't really fit the "nose job" part. Hence the reason my husband had gone into hiding.

Okay, maybe he didn't go into hiding, but he was certainly keeping his distance in public. He could read the stares as well as I could.

I took a deep breath and pulled out into the road. I guess I could explain to everyone who gave me that confused, pathetic look that my son had thrown a fast ball in the front yard and I didn't get my glove up fast enough, but I didn't feel like replaying that story over and over. It was a good one, though.

We were just tossing the ball in the front yard and I surprised him by firing one at him that left his glove smoking.

He looked at me with surprise and said, "Oh, is that how we're doing it?" in that typical teenager way.

I arrogantly mouthed off at him, "If you think you can take it!"

He wound up, let it fly, and...the last thing I remember is the ball coming straight at my face and then me laying flat out on the front yard. My kids, of course, freaked out.

I heard one of the little ones yell, "Mom's dying! Call dad!"

Then I heard my younger son muttering beside me, "Oh, Lord, please help Mama."

"I'll be okay, guys," I said, as tears streamed down my face. But all I could think about was that the ball had shoved my nose into my brain, causing severe damage; and now my kids were going to have a mom that drooled all over herself and couldn't remember their birthdays.

Oh, right. They already had that.

My husband rushed home and took me to the emergency room, only to be told that I should take pain reliever and put ice on it. *Thanks, doc; and how much will that cost me?*

So, after three days of Motrin, ice, and the occasional grimace when I tried to wash my face, I still looked like Sylvester Stallone at the end of "Rocky," (If you were born after 1975, just Google it). At any rate, I still looked bad...*real bad!*

The kids heard me grunt at my reflection in the rearview mirror (it's proven the more kids you have, the more you communicate with grunts and other indistinguishable sounds).

"Mama, I'm so sorry about hurting your face," said Karis, my aspiring professional baseball player.

"Honey, we've been through this. It's not your fault," I replied. "I'm fine. I've just cut you out of the will. No biggie."

"Mom, I'm serious!" He said. "Are you going to be all embarrassed to go out like...that?"

"Like what?" I asked. "Does this shirt look weird or something?"

"No, really," He said, "If you don't want to go out in public, I'll be glad to skip school today and just stay home."

I couldn't help laughing as his feeble attempt to play hookey. "Nice try, " I said, "but I'm fine." I thought for a minute and then added,

"In fact, I'm totally cool with it. People will see me and think, 'Whoa, that's one *bad donkey mama*, I'd better stay away from her!'"

The older kids in the car cracked up laughing, knowing that I said, "donkey" in lieu of another word for the posterior.

The younger kids just looked at me, wondering why on earth I would want to look like a donkey, and a bad one at that.

A King, A Prophet, and a Donkey
Donkeys aren't as dumb as you think they are. In fact, they probably know something you don't. Balaam can certainly attest to that fact, if he were around today. But he left a great story in the Bible about his experience with a phenomenal donkey. It's all written out in the twenty-second chapter of Numbers; and it's all about living without compromise.

Balaam was a prophet and had a heart for God. He truly did. But sometimes when we have a heart for God combined with a lust for the world it just doesn't make a great combination, kind of like Diet Coke and Mentos. Balaam was one of God's "it" guys. When he cursed something, it was cursed. When he blessed something, it was blessed. In other words, he was one of those people you would want following you on Twitter.

There was a king in Balaam's time named Balak and he ruled over Moab. Well, along came the Israelites and everywhere they went, they ruled. They overtook kingdoms, they claimed territory, and grew like crazy. And then they settled right on the outskirts of Moab, Balak's back porch. This scared the wits out of Balak and he sent for Balaam. He knew that if Balaam cursed the Israelites, they would no longer be a threat to Moab. He said, "Now come, I beg of you, curse this people for me, for they are too powerful for me. Perhaps I may be able to defeat them and drive them out of the land, for I know that he whom you bless is blessed, and he whom you curse is cursed" (Numbers 22:6). Sounds like a pretty desperate guy, right?

So Balak's people showed up at Balaam's house loaded down with lots of gifts and perks for Balaam to entice him to come curse the Israelites. And Balaam did the right thing. He didn't give them an answer right away and told them to stay for the night so he could talk to the Lord about it.

If experience has taught me anything, it's always give decisions at least twenty-four hours and make sure you consult with God before getting into anything. Good for Balaam!

That night, sure enough, God came to Balaam and Balaam explained the situation to Him (as if God didn't already know). Then God said to Balaam, "You shall not go with them, you shall not curse the people, for they are blessed" (Numbers 22:12).

So Balaam rose up the next morning and basically told the guys, "Hey, pack up your things and hit the road. God told me I couldn't go." So they thanked Balaam for letting them crash for the night and high-tailed it back to Moab.

Now, you would think that would be it, right? Wrong.

When God says, "No," He means "No." He doesn't mean, "Well, I'm not sure that would be a good idea, but maybe if you just work really hard and make some adjustments here and there it could work out for you." God's word always stands true and no modifications on our part are ever going to change that. Balaam knew this, but it's funny how the world can give you a sudden case of amnesia.

Balak was not going to be stopped. He sent more people to Balaam to implore him to come. This time, he didn't just send his "peeps," he sent noble princes—"more of them and more honorable than the first ones" (Numbers 22:15). He even sent word by them saying, "I will promote you to very great honor and I will do whatever you tell me; so come, I beg of you, curse this people for me." Balak was giving Balaam serious incentive to come do some cursing.

But good old Balaam, he did the right thing. He answered them saying, "If Balak would give me his house full of silver and gold, I cannot go beyond the word of the Lord my God, to do less or more." Now that should have been the last straw. It should have been like Trump saying, "You're fired!" That's it. No deal. Get out of here. But Balaam made his first mistake. He let them hang around. He told them to stay the night so he could talk to the Lord some more about it.

Seriously, Balaam? Was God not clear enough before? It's funny how the glow of riches can suddenly dim the instructions of God. The longer those noble princes hung out with him and the more they flashed their riches and talked about Balak's big promises, the more time Balaam had to consider a compromise. It's kind of like hanging out at the car lot. Pretty soon, you're going to get roped in to a sale.

That night, God put a test before Balaam. He said, "Look, Idiot," (okay, He didn't really say "Look, Idiot". That was my version of the text). He really said, "If those noble princes come call on you tonight, go ahead and go with them. But do NOT do anything without my say." They didn't call on him that night. But I'll tell you what *did* happen that night. Balaam probably laid awake in bed pondering all of those promises, considering all of those riches, dreaming about all of that power, and all the cool stuff he could do with it. The more time you have to think, the more time you have to mess up. And that's where Balaam messed up. He got up, saddled his donkey, and decided to go with those men of Moab, without God's permission.

It gets especially tough to make clear, godly decisions when we can see the goods we would get if we compromised,…just…a…little…bit. Scripture tells us to enter through the narrow gate—

"for wide is the gate and spacious and broad is the way that leads away to destruction, and many are those who are entering through it. But the gate is narrow (contracted by pressure) and the way is straitened and compressed that leads to life, and few are those who find it" (Matthew 7:13,14).

The wide road is the feel good road. It's the easy way, the just-enough-to-get-by way. And that's the road that most people take. But it always leads to destruction. If we're ever going to reach an abundant life, we need to get comfortable with being uncomfortable. It feels compressed sometimes, and contracted. But it's like the contractions we have when we're giving birth to a child. Sure, the pain is there. But so is the promise.

When we choose to live without compromise, we're willing to make the tough choices now to get to the promise later. Most people live for today, not for tomorrow. We live in a culture of compromise. In the Amplified Bible, whenever the word righteous is used, it is almost always preceded by the word, "uncompromisingly". That's what true righteousness is—refusing to compromise, being willing to stand firm in a world that goes with the flow. It's a rare thing indeed to find that person who is willing to stick to their guns, to live by their principles, to have the guts to obey God's commands and the boldness to claim God's promises. Sometimes, it's not even a person at all.

It's a donkey.

What's That Donkey Up To?
So there goes Balaam on his donkey, heading out to Moab with the cool crowd. I bet he had that gnawing feeling in the pit of his stomach, too. You probably know that feeling—'I shouldn't be here. This is not me. What am I doing?' Have you ever had that feeling? You know, when are trying desperately to rationalize why you are doing something, while your gut is telling you to turn and run? Well, I'm thinking that's what Balaam was going through. He knew better. He had principles. He just compromised them.

That's when God got mad. Scripture tells us "God's anger was kindled because he went, and the Angel of the Lord stood in the way as an adversary against him" (Numbers 22:22). Don't think that you can ever figure a way around God. When you choose to compromise God's direction, it's like an open invitation for adversity to come into your life.

God doesn't want adversity for your life, but He will certainly allow it if it's going to keep you from something destructive. I'm sure Balaam didn't intend to go curse the Israelites. In his mind, he was probably just going to check things out for a bit. That's how the spiral begins, with slow, steady compromises. God wants to bless you, but He can't bless your disobedience. Don't take the easy route. Stand firm in your conviction.

It's so easy to compromise. Balaam did it. But his donkey didn't—

"The donkey saw the Angel of the Lord standing in the way and His sword drawn in His hand, and the donkey turned aside out of the way and went into the field. And Balaam struck the donkey to turn her into the way" (Numbers 22:23).

Isn't it funny how our foolishness makes us blind? When you start to compromise your values and your principles, it makes you blind to the direction that God is giving you. Balaam was focused on his goods, not his God. That's why he couldn't see God's direction for his life even when it was smack-dab in the middle of his path. But his donkey did, and she turned aside. And as a result, she got the ever-lovin' poop smacked out of her!

When we choose to live by God's standards and draw the line, it's going to ruffle some feathers and rock some boats. I wish I could tell you that when you follow God's will for your life and stand up for what you believe, it's going to be all sunshine and roses; but my mama taught me never to lie. It's not going to be easy, and there will be plenty of people who won't understand you and even criticize you. Now, if they smack you on the bottom, that's another problem for another book.

Please understand. If God's way was easy, everyone would be following it. Like I said, we live in a culture of compromise. When you choose righteousness, you're waging war. But that's a good thing, 'cause you're on the winning team!

It's Smackdown Time!

www.hannahhelpme.com

As if one smack wasn't enough, that donkey had to go and get herself in trouble again!—

"the Angel of the Lord stood in a path of the vineyards, a wall on this side and a wall on that side. And when the donkey saw the Angel of the Lord, she thrust herself against the wall and crushed Balaam's foot against it, and he struck her again" (Numbers 22:24,25)

The path that leads to life is narrow. It's compressed. It's constricted by pressure. There's a reason for this. When God gets a hold of you and wants to do something amazing with your life, he's going to have to squeeze all the gunk out of you. The pride, the ego, the self-righteousness—it's all got to go. God can't do anything with your life until it's emptied out. And sometimes, that process can be painful; but when you come out the other side you are better off than you were when you went into it. God is great and God is good. He is powerful enough to get you where you need to be; and loving enough to sustain you through the process.

Balaam's donkey saw that the path was constricted. There was a wall on either side that kept her from passing through. When she responded by pushing up against one side, it crushed Balaam's foot. Of course, you already know what that fool went and did. He smacked her again! The process of taking bold steps in a wimpy world can sometimes be painful. The process can hurt, but the product is worth it.

But the smackdown wasn't over for that poor donkey. God's love for us is relentless. God continues trying over and over to give us direction and pull us back into the abundant life He has designed us for. He tried once more for Balaam. The next part of the passage tells us about it—

"the Angel of the Lord went further and stood in a narrow place where there was no room to run, wither to the right hand or to the left. And when the donkey saw the Angel of the Lord, she fell down under Balaam, and Balaam's anger was

kindled and he struck the donkey with his staff" (Numbers 22:26,27).

Whoa! Now, he has resorted to using his staff! He's intent on beating some sense into that donkey, even if the donkey is the only one with any sense to begin with. There will definitely be those times in life when all you can do is just fall on your face before God. You don't know which direction to turn. You're confused, discouraged, and at the end of your proverbial rope. But God is there. He has promised to never leave you nor forsake you. And He's good for it. When you humble yourself before God, He will exalt you when the time is right. And the time was right for that donkey. But first, she had to get a major whoopin'! Doesn't that seem to happen to us? Just when we think we can't take any more, we fall on our face before God and then things seem to turn from bad to worse.

I remember one day when it just seemed that things were going from bad to worse for me. The house kept getting messier the more I cleaned up. I was behind in my paperwork. And I didn't have anything in the house to make for lunch. After scouring the pantry, I finally found three boxes of macaroni and cheese and began preparing it for the kids. As I poured the noodles into the pot, an entire basket of toys fell over in the living room and spilled out all over the place. When I ran in to the living room to check it out, all the lights suddenly went out.

'Great!' I thought, 'now I have a blown fuse!"

As I turned to head down to the basement, I noticed a truck had pulled into our driveway and two men with hardhats on were coming around the side of the house. I went outside and said, "Excuse me, is there something I can help you with?'

"Well," said one of them in that characteristic Virginia drawl, "it looks like someone forgot to pay their electricity bill!"

Just when I thought it couldn't get worse, it did! Don't fall into that trap of thinking it's as bad as it can get. It's all a matter of perspective. I eventually called the electric company and worked out a deal where I could pay $100 over the phone and then pay off the rest of the bill throughout the next few months. (Yeah, did I mention that we only had $400 in the bank at the time?). I could have become discouraged and disappointed, but instead, I remember something welling up inside me. It was conviction. God was speaking to my spirit, telling me that He created me for more than just scraping by with cheap macaroni and cheese and unpaid bills. He had a bigger life planned for me. I dug my heels in that day and decided I was going to reach it, no matter how many boxes of macaroni and cheese I had to eat along the way. Sometimes God uses pain to pull us higher. It all depends on how you react to it. The donkey stayed obedient, in spite of his stinging backside. If you're dealing with a stinging backside, stay faithful. Keep your chin up. God says he will reward you with beauty for ashes and joy for despair, and He's good to His word. Rub out the pain and keep walking toward your dreams.

The Donkey is Delivered
God is good; and He is faithful to His promises. The donkey was punished for having common sense and integrity, and she was suffering because of it. Not one time, not two times, but three times she had to suffer for her obedience to God.

Then God does something crazy (as usual). Numbers 22:28 says that "the Lord opened the mouth of the donkey, and she said to Balaam, What have I done to you that you should strike me these three times?" Yep, that's right. The donkey talked! And it may be because of one too many viewings of Shrek, but I can never read this passage in scripture without hearing the voice of Eddie Murphy. The donkey talks back to Balaam and puts him in his place. Then after they exchange a few words, God does something else. He talks to Balaam directly and defends Eddie Murphy. I mean, the donkey.

"The Angel of the Lord said to him, Why have you struck your donkey three times? See, I came out to stand against and resist you, for your behavior is willfully obstinate and contrary before Me. And the ass saw Me and turned from Me these three

times. If she had not turned from Me, surely I would h
you and saved her alive" (Numbers 22:32,33)

How cool is that? Not only did God allow the ⟨ ⟩ to speak, but then God Almighty, the Creator of the heavens and the earth, spoke out in her defense. Sure, He called her an ass, but that just goes to show you that you don't have to be perfect to be used by God. He's not looking for perfect people. He's looking for obedient people who will live without compromise. Even if that means using an ass every once in a while!

God cares so much about righteousness, that He will honor and protect those who do what is right and live without compromise. He was even willing to honor and protect a donkey. How much more will He honor and protect you for your obedience? If you live with integrity, even when it hurts, God will use it in mighty ways. Not just to protect and guide you, but also to protect and guide those people who depend on you, just like Balaam depended on his donkey.

Keep being obedient to God, and He will give you a voice to proclaim Him and He will step out in your defense. He is your Protector and your Defender. You are His child; and, trust me, no one messes with His children and gets away with it.

There will always be opportunities to compromise—how you parent your children, care for your marriage, manage your home, perform at your workplace. Sometimes it seems too difficult to put in another day of effort, or too tempting to keep sticking to your values. But, remember, God has placed you in a divine role for a divine reason. He will raise you up and exalt you for His great and mighty purpose if you remain obedient. Your deliverance is at hand!

You don't need to be a puffed up prophet or a high-falutin' intellectual to be used by God (this may be a good time to tell you that "intellectual" came up twice on spell-check…just letting you know who you're dealing with here). All you need to be is you. Donkeys are simple. They follow God and they speak truth. All the time Balaam had thought his donkey was being bad; but the donkey was just being obedient. The world isn't going to roll out the red carpet when you decide to take your life up a notch and pour your heart and soul into it. It might even smack you upside the head! But do you want the abundant life? Or do you want to compromise? Are you willing to walk the narrow path or will you choose the wide road? It's up to you.

Donkeys are unconventional. They don't fit in. They stand out in a crowd. And when they open their mouths and start talking? Hoowee! You better watch out! That's the thing about donkeys. They're not out to impress anyone. They're just doing their job and living out their principles. And that's a rare thing indeed in today's world. Donkeys are determined. When the whole world is going one way, donkeys have the guts to turn around and go in the other direction.

Are you ready to be 100% obedient to God? Are you ready to live without compromise? Are you ready get into full-on "donkey mode" and be crazy blessed? If so, then I declare right now that a longing for righteousness is rising up within you. You will live choose to live without compromise, when you see the results and even when you don't! It takes boldness and courage to be fully obedient. In the name of Jesus Christ, you are putting aside fear and timidity and stepping into a life of full obedience. You will take the narrow road and, in due time, you will see a harvest of your righteousness that will take your breath away. I believe it. I declare it. Now live it.

CRAZY BONUS!

Are you getting the help you need to live the life you want?
Well, I've got a SURPRISE for you!
Use the code, "RESCUE20" and get over
HALF off the 21-Day Mom Rescue!
Just go to www.21daymomrescue.com and get
the help you need to live the life you want.

STEP 4

USE FIGHTIN' WORDS

Waking up my kids is no easy feat. The older they get, the more effort is required to get them out of bed. On Saturday mornings we all sleep in. For me, that means I get up around 7:30am. For my teenagers, it's more like 1pm. On school mornings, it usually takes a triple whammy. On the first attempt, I sing a nice little "good morning" song and turn on all the lights in their room. This usually results in groans and pillows over the head. I'm still not sure if it's the lights or the song. We'll say the lights.

On the second attempt, there is usually some type of threat associated with their refusal to get out of bed. Usually I threaten to sing a song again. This usually works. Hmmm…maybe it's not the lights.

On the third—and last—attempt, I sprout horns, my skin turns reptilian, fangs protrude out of my mouth, and I resort to emergency tactics. I've been known to play the drum set or even the vuvuzela. I still don't know how we got a vuvuzela. But, if you have teenagers that won't wake up, I strongly suggest purchasing one. The third attempt always works.

But it didn't this one day.

I tried over and over to get Kyler out of bed but he just wouldn't budge. Finally, I was busy cooking breakfast (or was it lunch?) when he stumbled into the kitchen. That boy looked like something the dog dragged in. His hair was sticking out everywhere, his eyes were half shut, and his face had this pale, greenish tint.

"Mama," he said, in a raspy voice. "I feel terrible."

Now, I'm a firm believer in the power of words. I believe everything is a confession of faith, and it can work for you or against you. I've found a way to prevent my kids from saying negative confessions over their lives by simply agreeing with them.

"Well," I said, "I agree with your confession."

Without hesitation, Kyler responded, "I wasn't talking to you. I was talking to that mom in my head who gives me the response I want and she said, 'Oh, baby, I'm so sorry.'"

The Power of Words

It's true. There is so much power in what you say. Remember that story about Balaam's donkey? Three times the donkey tried to knock Balaam off and prevent the evil from happening, but nothing changed—*nothing changed*—until that donkey opened its mouth and started talking. Did you get that? Because it's a major plot point. The donkey kicked, bucked, squirmed, and stopped, but nothing changed. However, when the donkey spoke, the story took a turn.

If you're ready for a plot point in your life that will knock your ever-lovin' socks off, then it's time to open your mouth and start talking! Words have power! If you realized how much power was in your words, you would be pleading along with King David, "Set a guard, O Lord, before my mouth; keep watch at the door of my lips" (Psalm 141:3). It's so true. Every word we say has creative power. So, the real question here is this: What are your words creating?

For years I felt stuck in my pursuits. I would do what all the experts suggested. I developed a vision for my life. I wrote down my goals. I broke my goals down into reachable steps. I followed through. I kept dreaming, kept working, kept trying. And it seemed like I just treaded water for years. I would push forward and then something would come along to pull me back. I would get $5000 and then get a bill for $4,985. It stayed this way for…so…long.

Then I did something that totally changed the course of my life. I opened up my mouth and started talking. Instead of just dreaming up goals, writing them down, and organizing all the steps to get there. I started speaking the goals. I started declaring them out loud! I would wake up in the morning with declarations on my lips and go to bed mumbling them to myself. When I would go walking, I would spend the entire time talking out loud and declaring my dreams as if they had already come to pass.

Now, if you've read this far, you already understand that you've got to be comfortable being outrageous if you're going to experience any success. Successful, prosperous people do not blend in. They rise above the masses. You've got to get yourself into a position where you are comfortable rising above the masses and standing out. God said that He wants you to be a city on a hill. A city on a hill stands out. It attracts attention. God wants to shine a light on you so other people can see what living in His blessing really looks like. And sometimes it's going to look foolish. But, remember, God uses the foolish to confound the wise.

I'm pretty sure I'm the woman in our neighborhood who people think is a bit off her rocker. I go walking and I'm praising God the entire time. I'm declaring His blessing over every area of my life and claiming visions He has given me. Sometimes, the goodness of God rises up in me and I just can't help it—I throw my hands up in praise! My husband is still looking for a more secluded place to live, but in the meantime, I've learned not to give a second thought about what people think. Okay, maybe I give a second thought every now and then, but not a third.

One day, when I first started doing this, I came home from walking and shared an idea with my husband.

"Honey," I said, "I'm sure every one in the neighborhood thinks I'm a whack job. I keep my mouth shut when I'm passing the kids at the bus stop and people walking their dogs, but the rest of the time, I'm talking on and on to God. But, I'm sure people think I'm talking to myself. I'm considering sticking your Bluetooth in my ear when I go walking so at least people think I'm talking to an actual person."

ɔoked at me with his best '*I'm about to set you ɩook* and said, "Why would you do that? What are you ɑfraid of?"

And, yes, he did set me straight that day.

If you're worried about how you look or what people think, you are operating under a fear of man; and Proverbs 29:25 tells us that "the fear of man brings a snare, but whoever leans on, trusts in, and puts his confidence in the Lord is safe and *set on high*."

There's that "set on high" thing again. Are you getting it? Before you can ever claim the power that comes from declaring your success, you've got to be comfortable with being uncomfortable. God doesn't want you to blend in. Crazy blessed people *never* blend in! He's not going to bless you so you can go crawl off somewhere and fit in. He's going to bless you so that others can see your good works and glorify Him (Matthew 5:16). He wants to set you on high as an example of the wondrous things that can happen when someone learns to throw away any self-consciousness and totally lean on, trust in, and put confidence in Him. Basically, he wants to use you as an example of how good He treats His kids.

You can't step into the blessing of God if you're holding on to the approval of man. It's one or the other. So, before we move on and talk about talking, get rid of the fear of man. It's a snare. It will trip you up and keep you from the abundance God has laid up for you.

Tapping into the method of speaking your success will test you in every way possible. You'll look foolish. You'll sound foolish. You'll feel foolish. After all, what sense does it make for a person to say, "I'm wealthy" when she has less than twenty bucks in her bank account? Or to say "I'm healthy" when the doctor has just given her a chronic diagnosis? It doesn't make sense, not in the earthly realm. But that's how God's kingdom operates.

So, if you're ready to leave the fear of man behind, get ready to open your mouth and shape your future!

Coming Undone!
I remember when I first became conscious of my words. I mean, *really* conscious of my words. I was shocked at how many times I uttered, or almost uttered, something negative. I was even more shocked at how much negative talk surrounded me. People are constantly complaining. They complain about the weather, their job, their homes, their kids, their lives, their churches, their friends, their enemies, you name it! Nothing is off limits when it comes to complaints and negative talk.

Isaiah certainly understood this. When he found himself in the presence of God, this is what he said:

"Woe is me! For I am undone and ruined, because I am a man of unclean lips, and I dwell in the midst of a people of unclean lips; for my eyes have seen the King, the Lord of hosts" (Isaiah 6:5).

This is the reason we become "undone." Have you ever felt like you were just falling apart? As if you were scattered and going nowhere fast? I firmly believe that this condition happens in our lives as a result of the words we speak. Isaiah was undone and ruined—not because of his circumstances, but because of the words he spoke over his circumstances. His lips were unclean and he knew it. And he lived in a society full of people who were talking the exact same way he was talking.

It's not easy to stand out, I understand that. But if you want to be crazy blessed, you're going to have to get comfortable with standing out. You were called to break free, not to blend in. When you dwell in the midst of people who like to complain, bicker, gossip, and all those other "unclean" things, it's going to take a lot of gumption to rise above and be different. But, Isaiah didn't even realize he wanted to be different until he found himself in the presence of God. Because his eyes beheld something amazing, he wanted his lips to follow suit. The best way to begin changing the words you say is to spend more time in the presence of God. That's where all changes are going to start, right there at the feet of God—reading His Word, listening to His heart, being filled with His Spirit. Suddenly, you'll become more aware of the words you speak and you will mold them to reflect the life that God wants you to live.

So Isaiah was stuck. Here he was in the presence of God Almighty, knowing full well that he did not have any right to be there. He had unclean lips. He had spoken negativity and nothing evil can exist in the presence of God (and, yes, negative talk is evil). What was he going to do? Well, God, in His mercy, was already on it.

"Then flew one of the seraphim [heavenly beings] to me, having a live coal in his hand which he had taken with tongs from of the altar; and with it he touched my mouth and said, Behold, this had touched your lips; your iniquity and guilt are taken away, and your sin is completely atoned for and forgiven." Isaiah 6:6,7

God saves the day once again! He takes one of the coals from the altar and touches Isaiah's lips with it. In that one act, all the iniquity and guilt is taken away. What you have or have not done up to this point is not important. It's what you do from here on out! Jesus himself gave His life on the cross for you. That was the altar! That one act cleanses you from all iniquity and guilt. One touch and you're clean! No matter how you have talked up to this point is irrelevant. What matters is how you are going to talk from now on. If God has saved your soul, let Him save your lips, too! That's where it all starts.

God's Holy Spirit is often symbolized as a fire. Let His Spirit invade your heart and purify your lips so you can start talking about the abundant life He has planned for you. That's holy fire, honey!

I remember one time I used my daughter's "lip plumper" lip balm. I didn't know about it at the time, but it was made with capsaicin, which is the compound that makes hot peppers, hot! I swiped that sucker on my lips and in about four seconds, they started burning like crazy! My lips were plumped all right, and they were on fire! I want you to be so conscious of the words you say that it's like you keep a burning hot lip plumper over your mouth—a Holy Spirit guard of fire so that no unclean talk can come out!

Who Are You Agreeing With?
There are two plans for your life—God's plan and Satan's plan. God wants you to have a crazy blessed life and Satan wants you to have a life that total destruction. It's all laid out very clear in scripture:

"The thief comes only in order to steal and kill and destroy. I came that they may have and enjoy life, and have it in abundance (to the full, till it overflows)." John 10:10

  That's what a crazy blessed life is all about! It's enjoying life and having everything in abundance, to the full, until it is overflowing in the lives of everyone who comes in contact with you. I want to have the kind of life that is so blessed that one touch or one word from me, and BAM…someone's life is dramatically improved.
  'Wow, Hannah,' you may be thinking. 'That's awfully prideful and arrogant.' You can think that if you want, but God's Word says that He wants to bless us so much that it spills out on everyone around us. When Peter would walk along the path, people who touched his robe would be healed. When Peter's shadow passed over people who were lame, they would jump up and start walking! That's the authority, power, and blessing He wants us to carry! He says that "In you will all the families and kindred of the earth be blessed [and by you they will bless themselves]" (Genesis 12:3).
  It's not arrogant and prideful to want to be blessed. It's God's will for our lives! Living a life of "just enough" is actually one of the most selfish things you can do because you're only focused on yourself, wanting "just enough" money to get by, or "just enough" home to fit your family, or "just enough" energy to make it through the day. But, here's the problem: God didn't put you here on this earth for "just you." He put you here to spread His glory and expand His kingdom. That can only happen when

you are blessed like crazy—so much so that is overflows on the lives of those around you.

That's fine if you have "just enough" money to feed yourself and your family. But what about the millions of children who go to bed hungry every night? Do you understand what I'm saying? Because nothing will have any impact from here on out if you do not grasp this extremely important concept: God wants you to be blessed like crazy! That is His covenant. You do no good for His kingdom at all when you live a "just enough" existence in a huge world that is broken and hurting. You are here to be blessed and spill those blessings out to a world in need. That is God's plan for your life.

Satan's plan, on the other hand, is completely opposite. He comes to steal, kill, and destroy; and he will stop at nothing to get it done. He wants you broke, sick, defeated, depressed, anxious, and all that other stuff that goes along with the curse. He is cursed and everything he does it cursed. But through Christ you are free of that! When He hung on the cross and said, "It is finished," He meant it! That curse is broken and you are free to live in abundance—both in heaven and here on earth.

Now, whose plan are you going to follow? Who are you going to believe? Because your plans and your beliefs will be shown through the words that come out of your mouth. If you are in agreement with God's plan for you, you will constantly be speaking His word over your life and your circumstances. If you are in agreement with Satan's plan, you will be speaking his lies. I may not have a penny in the bank, but if I say, "I'm broke," then I'm speaking a lie. Everything in opposition to God's word is a lie and His word tells me that the Lord is my shepherd and I shall not want (Psalm 23:1). It tells me that riches, honor, enduring wealth, and prosperity are with me (Proverbs 8:18). It tells me that the blessing of the Lord makes me rich and He adds no sorrow to it (Proverbs 10:22). Our circumstances can lie to us, but God never does. His word is truth. It tells me that He will meet all my needs according to His riches in Christ Jesus. And if I have honored Him and lived according to His commands, then I can count on Him to come through. My bank account may tell me I have nothing, but God says that I am wealthy and it's on its way. If I confess, "I'm broke," then I'm agreeing with Satan. If I confess, "I'm wealthy," then I'm agreeing with God.

'Well, that doesn't make any sense, Hannah,' you may be thinking. 'Saying that I'm wealthy when I don't have a red cent sounds more like a lie to me.'

That's because we have been so trained to believe in our circumstances instead of the God Who reigns over our circumstances. Everything is a test. God is searching all over the place to find someone He can bless like crazy. When He finds a heart that believes in His plans even when they can't find a single trace of it in their lives, that's when the storehouses of heaven fly open and blessings pour out!

"He who breathes out truth shows forth righteousness (uprightness and right standing with God), but a false witness utters deceit." Proverbs 12:17

Look carefully. When you "breathe out truth" you are confessing the Word of God. John 17:17 says, "Your word is truth." So when you are speaking what God says about you, then you are speaking the Truth. Not the truth that you can see with your eyes and touch with your fingers, but the real Truth. And when you continually believe and speak this Truth, it is eventually manifested in your life. Or you can speak a false witness, which is confessing Satan's plans for your life—defeat, despair, lack, sickness, all of that stuff that goes under the category of the curse. Revelation 12:9 tells us that Satan is the deceiver of the whole world. And if he can get you to start believing and confessing his plans for your life, then he's sucked you right in. You've got to keep confessing Truth even in the middle of a reality that seems to be in direct opposition.

Everything in David's circumstances told him he was going to be defeated by Goliath. Goliath was over ten feet tall. He had a sword and a spear. His armor was practically impenetrable. His shield alone probably weighed more than David! David was a young guy with nothing but a sling in his hand. But David had the faith to believe in God, rather than his circumstances. He told that giant, "Today the Lord will hand you over to me and I'll kill you and cut off your head (I Samuel 17:46). What sense does that make? David didn't even have a sword! How was he going to cut off Goliath's head? In reality, it didn't make a bit of sense. But David wasn't operating in reality. He was operating by faith in God's kingdom. And we all know how that story turned out. David knocked him out with a slingshot, and then used Goliath's own sword to cut off his head.

No matter what challenge you are facing, or what giant is threatening you, don't agree with it! Don't let it intimidate you! God Almighty is fighting your battles. And when you speak words in agreement with Him, no force on earth can withstand you. God will even use your enemies and your challenges to work in your favor. David would not have been able to cut off Goliath's head if Goliath hadn't come at him with a sword. Don't fear the challenge before you. In God's kingdom, it's nothing but hot air. It's Satan blowing smoke. But, remember, you have the breath of God going in your favor. God will make your enemies your footstools if you stay in agreement with Him. There is a war waging around you. Circumstances constantly rise up to try to steal your faith and defeat you. You've got to arm yourself with the Word of God and start speaking those fightin' words!

Your Words Are Your Weapons
Your words are your weapons. Keep saying that. Keep believing that. *Your words are your weapons!* Winning in life is not about finding the right breaks, knowing the right people, or getting the right education. It's about believing what God says and then saying it yourself. He is the one Who fights your battles, lines up the right breaks, puts the right people in your path, and gives you the necessary life education to reach the "good, pleasing, and perfect" plan that He has for your life (Romans 12:2). But how can you speak it if you don't know it? You've got to dig into the Word and get what's coming to you!

When my daughter got her acceptance letter from the college she chose to go to, she told everyone. She announced it at church. She even bought a t-shirt from the college and was wearing it all over town. When people asked her about her plans after high school, she was quick to tell them about the college she was going to and what she was planning on studying. She spouted off her plans to every ear that would listen. Even the poor guy behind the counter at Bed, Bath, and Beyond had to listen to why she was purchasing a lap desk and a mattress pad for her new college jaunt! She was excited about her new adventure and was talking about it constantly.

What if she had never received that acceptance letter? Do you think she'd be jabbering on about it left and right? No way! She may be wishing and hoping, but she wouldn't have the confidence to proclaim it until she had that letter in her hands.

You already have your acceptance letter. It's the Word of God. He has accepted you and wants to do an amazing work in your life.

"Even as [in His love] He chose us [actually picked us out for Himself as His own] in Christ before the foundation of the world, that we should be holy (consecrated and set apart for Him) and blameless in His sight, even above reproach, before Him in love." Ephesians 1:4

That's right, honey. You're in the big leagues now! Before you were even a twinkle in your mama's eye, He chose you and accepted you. In His extreme love, He set you apart and put you above reproach. Reproach means "disapproval or disappointment." He wants to give you a life that is above any disappointment, a life of abundance. This is our hope! That no matter what our lives may look like right now, God created us for prosperity, health, joy, and abundance; and when we stay faithful to that plan, He will come through. Romans 5: 5 tells us that this hope "does not disappoint." How incredible is that? When we keep fighting with our faith and get our words in alignment with His words, He will always come through! He will not disappoint us.

You have your acceptance letter. But if you don't read it, you'll never have the confidence to believe it. If Kelsey had received that acceptance letter but never took the time to open the envelope and read what was inside, she wouldn't have the confidence to talk about her future in such a positive way. She may wish and hope that it would come through, but without that letter in hand, she wouldn't have that unshakable certainty.

You can't talk up a fight if you don't have the confidence to back it up. And that confidence can only come from the Word of God. And it is unshakable! This book is not your manual to get crazy blessed. It's your guide. The Bible is your manual! If you're not taking the time and energy to dig into God's Word to find out the truth about who you are and what you have, you'll never have the confidence to claim it.

One Step Forward, Two Steps Back
Have you ever felt that you stepped out in faith and started confessing God's Word over your situation and nothing…ever…changes? I hear you! I've been through the fire enough times to understand where you're coming from. And that's just what it is—a holy fire that God is using to purify you and see if you are strong enough to bear the weight of His blessing.

Whether you realize it or not, blessing carries weight, and you need training to be strong enough to bear it. If you don't have the skills to manage $100, you'll never be able to manage a million. If you don't have the skills to manage a 1000 square foot home, you'll never be able to manage a 5000 square foot home. Abundance just magnifies what is already in you. If you operate by greed and lack, you'll just have more greed and lack. If you operate by gratitude and generosity, you'll just have more gratitude and generosity. Those "fire tests" that God puts you through is putting you in a position for you to bear the weight of abundance. It's training your muscles to carry more blessing in your life.

God's Word tell us that we should get excited when we are being tested through trials and temptations, and being tempted to agree with our circumstances. It's all a test. God is building your muscles to bear the weight of blessing. The stronger the muscle, the bigger the blessing. Ever feel tempted to get anxious over that child who is rebelling? That's when you stand firm and say, "As for me and my house, we will serve the Lord!" Ever feel tempted to get stressed out about that bill you can't pay? That's when you claim God's promise that you will "lend and not borrow." Tempted to gripe at your spouse? That's when you claim that "the law of kindness is on your lips."

I know it can be tempting to give in to your circumstances, but the temptations are just tests. Consider it push-ups for your faith! Sure, it's tough! But you're tougher, because you can do all things through Christ Who gives you strength. You've got the potential in you, and God's holy fire is going to refine you, test you, and prove you worthy of carrying the weight of a crazy blessed life. You've got it in you to do one more rep. I know it!

Racehorses wear blinders so they don't get distracted by what's going on around them. Their owners know they will only reach the prize if they have their focus on the goal ahead of them. Satan will keep trying to distract you from your blessing, from the Truth that God says about you. Remember, Satan is a liar. God speaks Truth. If you're really serious about getting blessed like crazy, you're going to have to become blind to the distractions and deaf to the voices that keep telling you lies. You know those voices—they whisper, "It'll never happen," "You've blown it," "That situation will never turn around." Those are lies. Just respond with, "No, thank you. I'm going to believe what God says about my future!" Then put your blinders on, stick your ear plugs in, and head for the prize.

"[You should] be exceedingly glad on this account, though now for a little while you may be distressed by trials and suffer temptations, So that [the genuineness] of your faith may be tested, [your faith] which is infinitely more precious than the perishable gold which is tested and purified by fire." I Peter 1:6,7

See that? God is testing you with fire. Are you going to give under pressure, or are you going to stand firm? The choice is yours. Get excited when the tests come because God is preparing you for abundance. Don't take one step forward in faith, and then if things don't start working out in your favor, take two steps back. That's what the Israelites did and it kept them wandering in the wilderness for forty years. You've got to have faith to make the journey. For some, it might take 40 days; for others, 40 years. And, unfortunately, there will be many that will never see their promise become a reality at all—not because God can't do it, but because they don't have the faith to believe that He really can. It's all up to you.

I'm going to be honest with you. God's promise of a crazy blessed life is for everyone, but not many are going to take Him up on it. It takes guts! It takes perseverance! Few are able to keep the faith in the middle of the fire. Are you one of them? If you've stuck with me this far, then I'm thinking you are! So, let's get after it! Anyone can have faith when things work in their favor. That's not faith at all. That's just common sense. When things take longer than they should, or don't turn out like you planned, that's when God is at work to prepare you for something greater. Keep the faith and keep speaking God's Word over your life.

Ain't Gonna Make Sense
Nope, it won't. Faith doesn't make a bit of sense in real life. There's a physical realm, the stuff we can experience with our senses; and there's a spiritual realm, the stuff we experience with our faith. Here's the coolest part—the physical realm is under the authority of the spiritual realm. Everything that you see around you began as an idea—everything! That chair you're sitting in? It began as an idea. That car you drive around? It began as an idea. The phone you hold in your hand, the lamp you turn on, those shoes you're wearing—they all began in the spiritual realm as a creative idea. When anything is created, it is first created in the invisible realm and then makes it way to the visible realm.

That's how God set it up. He created the universe and then spoke it into manifestation. Because we have God's Spirit in us, we have the power to do the very same thing in our lives. We have creative power! According to Romans 4:17, we serve a God Who "gives life to the dead and speaks of the nonexistent things that [He has foretold and promised] as if they [already] existed." And we have that same power. We can take the promises He has laid out for us in His Word and claim them as Truth. We have the right to speak of them as if they already existed. Because in God's kingdom, they already do.

The Word of God tells us that the weak should say, "I am strong" (Joel 3:10). The poor should say, "I am rich." The sick should say, "I am well." Sure, anyone could give in to their circumstances and begin to agree with them. But nothing will ever change if you do that. You will stay stuck! We are called to rise above and "call the end from the beginning," just as God does. What "end" do you want to see in your life? Because you're going to have to call it from the beginning. Do you want to see healing? Say that you're healed. Do you want to see blessing? Say that you're blessed. Do you want to see strength? Say that you're strong. If you want to see breakthroughs happen in your life, they will always start in the invisible and become manifested in the visible. And you will usher them in with your unwavering faith and your fightin' words!

Nothing about the faith walk makes sense to those who are agreeing with their circumstances. But you weren't called to "make sense." You were called for abundance! You were called for freedom! You were called to prosper! And you're going to have to start saying some fightin' words if you want to make it through the fire and get to your Promise.

What Fruit are You Growing?
In a house we used to live in, my neighbor had two beautiful trees in his front yard. One summer, Kelsey, who was just a little girl at the time, said, "Mama, why doesn't he ever pick that fruit and eat it? It all just falls on the ground and he rakes it up and throws it away." Now, that wouldn't make sense to anyone,

ot a little girl. Why would a person waste perfectly
But, what she didn't know was that those two
es were crabapple trees. And if you've ever tried to
eat a crabapple, you would understand why the only thing
they're good for is the compost pile. They're way too sour to eat.
Once, when I was little, a friend dared me to eat one. I took one
bite. My face shriveled up like a raisin and I spit that nasty thing
out! That was one dare I didn't follow through on (and probably
the only one!).

When it comes to words, you truly do become what you
speak. Your words are so powerful! When they come out of your
mouth, it's as if each word is a seed that is planted in your life.
When you speak abundance, you reap a harvest of abundance.
When you speak lack, you will reap a harvest of lack. You can
use words to build; or you can use words to break. It's your
choice.

*"Death and life are in the power of the tongue, and they
who indulge in it shall eat the fruit of it [for death or life]."
Proverbs 18:21*

See? Didn't I tell you that words were powerful? The
words you speak contain the power of life and death. It all
depends on how you use them. If you choose to speak words of
scarcity ("I don't know how I'm going to pay the bills this
month!") then that's exactly what you are going to grow in your
life—more scarcity. If you speak words of overwhelm ("I can't
handle this!"), then you're going to reap more overwhelm. All of
these negative words are in agreement with Satan's will for your
life; and remember, he comes to steal, kill, and destroy. That's
why these words are death words—they cause the promise that is
within you to die. All the abundance that God had planned for
you since before the foundations of the earth were laid—the
financial prosperity, the fulfilling relationships, the health and
longevity in your body, the happy home life—die a slow,
miserable death because of the curse words you speak over them.

Did you think curse words were just those four-letter choice words that are bleeped out occasionally? No such thing! Curse words come in all shapes and sizes. Check them out:

- This situation is never going to turn around.
- There's always more month than money.
- My kid is never going to straighten up.
- We've just fallen out of love.
- This house is just too small.
- My children never follow directions.
- I can't keep up with anything.
- I'm sick and tired.
- I'm limited because of my _____ (fill in the blank with your own label).

Do you see what I mean? Many people spout out curse words all the time and never even realize it! But every single word is a seed. What fruit are you growing in your life? If you want to grow crabapples, then keep planting crabapple seeds. Eventually, your life will be fit for nothing more than the compost pile! But, I know you were meant for more. You have greatness within you! God has ordained you to receive abundant blessings. You can only receive these when you change your words around and start speaking life over situations. The Word of God has power! And He promises that His Word will always accomplish its purpose.

"So is my word that goes out from my mouth: It will not return to me empty, but will accomplish what I desire and achieve the purpose for which I sent it." Isaiah 55:11

When the Word of God comes out of our mouth, it goes to work, fulfilling its purpose. Start speaking the promises of God and watch the fruit that begins to grow in your life. It's amazing! But, remember, we have the creative power of God because His Spirit abides in us. Your word will also not return to you empty.

It will always result in a harvest. It just depends on what you want to harvest in your life.

Start speaking the Word of God. Start speaking the reality of your dreams and visions that He has given you. Bite your tongue when you are tempted to curse your future. Your words will always bear fruit. Let's make it something a little more appetizing than crabapples, okay? I know you can do this! God would not have put a dream in your heart and a vision in your mind if He did not intend to accomplish it, Keep dreaming, keep believing, and keep planting "word seeds" of greatness.

I declare right now that God is opening up abundance before you. It's time to focus on God's plans for you, to prosper you and bless you so wildly that those blessings spill out on every person and every situation in your life. It's time to speak God's Word over your circumstances, so that the storehouses in heaven burst forth and blessings and breakthroughs pour out into your life. I declare right now that when you speak Truth and step by faith and not by sight, unseen forces will rush to your aid and bring blessing from the invisible to the visible. You will go through the fire. Your faith will be tested. And you will rise up in victory to step into your Promised Land!

CRAZY BONUS!
Are you living under a lie of labels?
Watch this FREE video and find out!
Click on the link <u>RIGHT HERE</u>, or visit
www.hannahkeeley.com/blog//labels

STEP 5
QUIT BEING A CHEAP COPY

Our family really gets in to dressing up. We love Halloween because it gives us an excuse to dress up and take it out in public. About mid-October, we always make a trip to the thrift store to see what we can collect for our costumes. On this one trip, Kelsey didn't have anything planned, but was coming along to scope out the possibilities. She was 19 at the time; but in our family, age has never stood in the way of dressing up.

We were quickly filling our cart with various options—a frilly white nightgown Klara's outfit, an army jacket for Korben, and some shiny pants for Kenna to be a pirate. That's when I heard Kelsey holler from across the store.

"Mama!" she yelled. "Come here and look!"

I put back the "Huggy Bear" velvet fedora that Karis wanted to get, and walked over to where Kelsey was shopping.

"What is it?" I asked.

Kesley held up two shiny pairs of pants. One was pink and the other green and both had enormous legs that tapered down around the ankles. They could have easily passed as "Aladdin" costumes.

"How cool are these?" she said. "I can get both and Katie and I can dress up as genies this year."

"Those are perfect!" I said, and put them in the shopping cart.

On the way home, Kelsey and I talked about the other items we would need for the costumes. We would have to get some sheer fabric to cover their faces and we could use tank tops and create really big sleeves with some other type of fabric. We could even get some jewels and sequins to decorate them. The outfits were really coming together by the time we got home. As soon as we walked inside, Kelsey hollered for Katie to come see the surprise. Katie came running downstairs and into the kitchen where Kelsey was standing with a shopping bag.

"Okay," Kelsey said, "I've already got our costumes this year and you're going to love it." For dramatic effect, she slowly began pulling the pants out of the bag.

She then began slowly saying, "This year, we're going to dress up as—"

Before she could finish the statement, Katie took one look at the pants and said, "M.C. Hammer!"

You're an Original

I always find it amazing that as many kids as I have, each one is dramatically unique. Genie pants to one girl are M.C. Hammer pants to another! And just like our kids are different, we are different, too. When God made you, He made an original. And if you conform to the masses, you are not only living with less than the best, but you are also denying the world of the gift that's within you. Quit being a cheap copy of someone else, and have the confidence to step into the unique glory of being you! God made you the way He made you for a reason. The world needs what you've got. So, if you're going to be anything, be yourself! Anyway, conformity always comes back to kick you in the fanny.

I remember the day I learned this lesson. A friend of mine asked me to come along with her to a furniture store to check out a dining room table they wanted to purchase. I packed up our two little ones and headed out there with her. When I walked in, I was floored with all the beautiful pieces of furniture. For a woman whose home was filled with nothing but cast-offs and charity store finds, it was like taking a sugar-deprived kid into a candy store. After seeing such beautiful furniture, how could I ever go back to my rickety dining room table with peeling paint that seats four and my mattress pushed up against the wall with an old quilt pinned on the wall like a headboard?

I was eyeing this one solid pine extended headboard with drawers, lights, mirrors, and all the bells and whistles, and I began to drool over it. Literally. I'm pretty sure, a stream of drool fell out of my mouth onto one of the drawers. No sooner did I caress the molding on the headboard and moan, "Oh, yeah, baby! That's what I'm talking about!" when one of the salespeople came up to me.

That's when I should have run.

But, I didn't.

He slapped the side of the headboard and asked, "You like this baby?"

I didn't want to tell him, but "like" was not enough to describe my emotions toward this seductive piece of furniture. "Lust" was more like it. Straight-up, solid, unabashed LUST!

I replied, "Yes! I do! It's gorgeous!" (sidenote: telling a salesman you love an item is not always the smartest buying tactic!)
He said, "We can deliver it to you today if you want."

'Seriously?' I thought. 'That gorgeous piece of furniture is going to go in my house?' I was sure it would fit right in with my frayed wicker basket that holds my books and the old fiberboard dresser my husband had when he was in high school. It still had Snoopy sticker residue that I couldn't remove (I didn't know about Goo Gone back then).

Then, just for kicks, I looked at the price tag: $2,995! I laughed out loud.

"I don't have that kind of money, but thanks anyway," I said, and started to walk away…(if only I had just kept walking!!)

The salesman piped up, "Well, why don't you let me see if you can get it on credit? Then you can just pay a little bit each month. Surely, you could do that! That's how everyone gets furniture for their homes. No one pays full price up front."

'Hmmmm…credit?' I thought. 'What was this cool, new thing called "credit? I would have to find out what this mysterious "credit" thing was all about and why everyone seemed to be doing it except me.'

It was like taking a soon-to-be drug addict and showing him some methamphetamines and saying, "Look, see? Everyone's doing it! Give it a try!"

After a few phone calls, the salesman came to me grinning like a Cheshire cat.

"Great news!" he said! "I got you approved for the entire amount. We can deliver it to you today and you don't even need to put anything down."

It was as if the heavens parted and I heard the angels singing in chorus! Looking back, I'm pretty sure that sound was Satan laughing his head off! I took the bait, signed on the line, and sealed my fate. It wasn't until later I found out just how expensive conformity really is.

The High Cost of Conformity
There is a drive in all of us to conform. It seems so much safer and comfortable there—in conformity. You're not alone and no one is looking at you like you've lost your mind. But the reality is that the vast majority of people today are living inferior lives, far below their capabilities. So if you're conforming to the masses, what you're really doing is living your life with your standards set on the lowest common denominator. But there is nothing low or common about God. He is extravagant and abundant. Scripture tells us that no eye has seen and no ear has heard of the wonders that our God can do. And, here's the shocker: He wants to do these wonders through you! So if you really want to live out God's greatness in your life, then you've got to get comfortable with being a bit…outrageous! I love how Paul put it when he was talking to the people in Rome:

> *"Do not be conformed to this world (this age), [fashioned after and adapted to its external, superficial customs], but be transformed (changed) by the [entire] renewal of your mind [by*

its new ideals and its new attitude], so that you may prove [for yourselves] what is the good and acceptable and perfect will of God, even the thing which is good and acceptable and perfect [in His sight for you]. Romans 12:2

Today, we live in a culture where right is wrong, wrong is right, and moral behavior is as subjective as what type of sauce you prefer with your pasta (I like marinara).

We live on slippery slopes today. The standards that God laid out for us are terribly compromised. And if you stand up for what's right and speak truth in the midst of lies, you're thought of as a lunatic, a fanatic, or both. Here's a tip: If you are fitting in and not stepping on any toes, then there's a huge chance you are conforming.

That doesn't mean we are supposed to go around with a "judgy, wudgy" attitude and point fingers at all the sinful people. Truth is, we're all sinful. And it's nothing but the grace of God that saves us from that sin and allows us to live in freedom and forgiveness. And it is because of this grace that we should strive to pursue righteousness. We want to be like Christ because of the mercy He has shown us. We can love and accept people, without loving and accepting the sin that is so rampant in our culture.

I'm going to go full "mama" on you here and tell you that even if everyone around you seems to be doing it, that doesn't make it right. I don't care how many weeks "Shades of Gray" stayed at the top of the bestseller list. There are no gray shades about it. Right is right and wrong is wrong. All you need to do is just go to the "Phlip Test" to see what makes the cut. That's what we call the bar we use to judge what our family allows in our eyes, ears, and minds, and it can be found in Philippians 4:8—

"For the rest, brethren, whatever is true, whatever is worthy of reverence and is honorable and seemly, whatever is just, whatever is pure, whatever is lovely and lovable, whatever is kind and winsome and gracious, if there is any virtue and excellence, if there is anything worthy of praise, think on and

weigh and take account of these things [fix your minds on them]." Philippians 4:8

God doesn't set boundaries because He wants you to be boring. He sets them because He wants you to be blessed. When we live righteously, we open doors for God to bless us in extreme ways.

But don't think refusing to conform is all about checking off the items on your list of righteousness. Sure, God wants us to live righteous lives, but He also wants us to live in abundance. We can live right—refuse to gossip, go to church, pray before meals, give to charity, and sponsor a kid in Uganda. But, there is a danger in finding comfort there. God wants us to always be progressing and growing. He never said He wants *you* to be good. He said that *His plans* are good, pleasing, and perfect. He wants you to get beyond good. He wants you to live boldly, to stretch your faith, to strive for more. His plans are for an abundant life, a life of "more than enough." If we get content with good, we've missed the point of not conforming.

Tats or No Tats?

Many people have the wrong impression of nonconformity. They immediately conjure up images of tattooed midriffs, plugged earlobes, and pierced tongues. Not so. C'mon, let's think a little deeper here, okay? Some of my best friends have tattoos, plugs, and piercings and they are on fire for God. And some of my best friends wear skirts down to their ankles, buttoned-up collars, and refuse to cut their hair and they are on fire for God, too.

Just like God told Samuel, an Old Testament prophet, "Man looks on the outside. God looks on the heart." He revealed this to Samuel when it was time to anoint a new king of Israel and He directed Samuel to a little shepherd boy, the youngest and smallest in his family. Samuel took one look at this tiny, inexperienced kid, and said, "Seriously, God?...Seriously?" But upon God's direction, he anointed him to be king. This kid's name was David and he grew to become the greatest king Israel ever had. The reason? He pursued God with all his heart and never, ever conformed!

There was one time, during David's reign, when the entire country was having a huge party and celebrating a victory. King David tore off his robes and danced in the street in an ephod! Now, if you don't know what an ephod is, just think of your grandma's kitchen apron—with nothing underneath! But, please don't think of your grandma actually wearing it that way. An image like that cannot be easily scrubbed from the mind. Great, now I said it. It's already out there. So sorry.

So, there goes David, dancing with the stars and flapping his butt cheeks in the wind. I mean, I've heard of Spirit-filled worship, but this beats all! It kind of reminds me of Times Square on New Years Eve. But, hey, if people can get that excited over a new year, then they can certainly get excited about a victorious God, right? David certainly understood this principle! And, my, oh, my, did that breeze feel good!

Okay, just to clarify, I am NOT telling you to go dance down Main Street in your underwear. However, if you live in New York City, that's an entirely different matter. I hear that behavior could probably pass as normal.

The point with King David is that he was willing to live in extreme. He wasn't about to conform! When he finally simmered down long enough to come back inside, his wife basically told him, "Oh, no, you did NOT just dance around in your tighty whiteys! That is SO embarrassing. You're a king, for crying out loud! And you're dancing around like some kind of South Beach stripper, letting all the girls check out your goods!" Okay, maybe I paraphrased it a bit, but the point still comes across loud and clear. She condemned his actions.

Then David pipes up and says something like, "Yo, Woman! I ain't parading around for all the babes to check me out. I'm dancing before my God, so get over it!" And he probably just stayed in his ephod for a while, traipsing through the house, just to get on her nerves. No doubt about it, David was a true blue nonconformist!

Do the Opposite
One of my mentors told me once to figure out what everyone else is doing and do the opposite. Pretty good advice! Think for a minute about where the masses are headed. Most people are just stumbling through life, stressed-out, in debt, and out of shape. It's rare that you find someone who is truly successful. Most people are just walking zombies, going along with life, digging themselves further and further in the same old ruts, and not knowing what it's like to truly live an abundant life.

The facts speak for themselves. Approximately 70% of women are on some type of anti-anxiety medication. The average American household carries a debt of over $54,000. Over a third of Americans are considered obese, and that doesn't even figure in the number of people who are out-of-shape and suffering from poor health. It's obvious that the masses are not on a very prosperous path.

But this isn't anything new. Scripture told us about this phenomenon a long time ago. Remember the wide and narrow pathways? Think about it, "…wide is the gate and spacious and broad is the way that leads to destruction." (Matthew 7:13). If you hear the words, "Everyone's doing it, " that should be a signal that it's that "Wide Road Mentality" that Jesus is talking about. If it looks easy and doesn't require much thought, time, or effort, then you can be sure it's headed for destruction.

I've figured out something pretty insightful about the wide and narrow paths. The wide road always starts out smooth and easy. It's so easy and simple to get into debt. All you have to do is check the box on the application or click a button on the computer screen. It's easy and simple to get out of shape. All you have to do is, well, nothing! Just sit around and eat whatever you want. It's easy and simple to let your marriage fall apart. Just ignore it entirely. Do you see why it's such a wide road? It's smooth, spacious, easy-peasy. But here's what happens to that wide road. It starts getting pretty bumpy after awhile. It's not so smooth and spacious anymore. People are elbowing you left and right and you can no longer see where you're headed. It's overgrown with strangling vines that wrap around you and gnarled limbs that trip you up. Destruction soon sets in.

But the road that leads to life is different. The gate is narrow, so narrow you can hardly fit. You have to dump all your pride and your ego in order to get through it. I remember watching an episode of "The Andy Griffith Show" in which Andy made this remark about Barney, his deputy: "That boys weighs about 100 pounds, and I swear 50 of it is proud."

That's how it is with most people. We can't dump our pride long enough to get on the right path in life. We so want to cling to our own cleverness. We long to be right and get our own way. Pride comes with a hefty price tag. You've got to dump the ego if you want to fit through the gate.

Then after you get through the gate, the pathway is straight and constricted. Every day seems to be an exercise in saying "no" to selfish desires and making the choice to do the hard thing—exercising when you'd rather just crash on the sofa, putting the shoes back on the shelf instead of whipping out the credit card, disciplining your child when you would just rather forget about the whole incident. But then something amazing happens to the pathway. It suddenly becomes wide and smooth. Those tough choices you made suddenly begin to pay off—you have more energy and can outlast the kiddos, you're totally debt-free and you have plenty of money in the bank, your kids are responsible and respectful. Suddenly, that constricted road has become spacious, peaceful, and easy. And there's plenty of room because you have outsmarted the masses. You have decided to take the narrow path and it paid off—big time.

Finally Comfortable

I don't think there was ever a time in my life when I conformed, although I tried, really, really hard. As a little kid, I didn't conform at all. I was five and a half feet tall in the fourth grade. Try conforming when all the other kids in your class come up to your armpits! Mama still has an old video of me at my kindergarten picnic. She panned down the entire line of kids and then came to one girl who was about a head taller than all the rest and was facing backwards. The worst part of the whole thing was that we all had to hold on to a long rope as we walked toward the picnic shelter. I was the tall, lanky, clueless girl walking backward with a dazed and confused look on her face!

As I got a little older, Mama thought it would help if I took a dance class with other girls. I was about a month in before I even figured out it was a dance class. I just thought Mama dressed me up in a tutu and sent me into a room to jump around for an hour. She finally pulled me out when the teacher advised her to have me transferred to a "special" class where I can get more personalized attention.

Then Mama tried music lessons. I remember a black clarinet, some shiny buttons, and licking a wooden thing on the mouthpiece. That's about it. Mama soon gave up on wind instruments and moved me to the string section. I believe it was my fourth violin lesson when Mama came in and saw me banging the piano keys with my horsehair bow screaming, "I can't learn this thing!!" That was my last lesson, too.

Things coasted along for a while until I hit middle school. All of a sudden there were real desks and lectures and books, and my mind drifted off in a thousand different directions. Day after day, I had to bring notes home for my parents to sign and they all said the same thing, "Hannah doesn't pay attention in class." One note said, "Hannah started a food fight in the cafeteria." Ahh, those were good times! That food fight was one of the redeeming qualities of middle school. The rest of the stuff bored me to the point of nausea.

I remember one day getting a sealed envelope to take home for my parents to sign. It was a lot different than the weekly notes, but it was just as anxiety provoking. After stalling as long as possible, I finally handed the envelope over to my parents. When they opened it Daddy hit the roof! It was a notice that they were placing me in "special needs" classes. Meanwhile, memories of tutus and ballet slippers flooded through Mama's head.

Well, Daddy wasn't going to stand for it. He marched right to that school and demanded that something be done. I just waited in the car, imagining that Daddy was walking in like Dwayne "The Rock" Johnson, and giving all those teachers a couple of 1-2 punches. Then he would pull open the gray metal filing drawers, tear up all my tests and records, and say (very loudly, maybe with a bit of a southern drawl), "My baby ain't going to take these classes! In fact, she ain't gonna take any classes at all! That darlin' of mine is gonna come home, watch TV, and play every single day, and you can't do a darn thing about it. No one puts baby in the corner!" Then he would walk out of the school, into the sunset, jump in his car after sliding over the hood, and we would ride out of the parking lot, squealing tires the whole way. It would be just like when Ferris Bueller drove out of the high school parking lot in that "choice" Ferrari.

Well, that's how I imagined it.

What really happened was Daddy asked them to have me tested to see if I truly qualified for special needs classes. They did. When the results came back, I went from special needs classes to advanced studies. Imagine that! There was something inside after all, but no one could tap into it! I also went from Ds and Fs, to As and Bs (until I took Driver's Ed, but that's an entirely different story). My grades improved astronomically and I even ended up being one of the top performing students when I hit high school. I believe I was #4 in the graduating class. Okay, there were only 27 of us, but it's still pretty remarkable. The food fights didn't stop, though. Teachers loved me. Lunch ladies feared me.

Sometimes I think that's how all of us are. I don't mean we are all out there with a penchant to start food fights. What I mean is that we all are walking around with genius buried deep within us. There is so much inside, but so often we just end up conforming. God's beautiful masterpiece that He designed within us is left unpainted. You are you for a reason. You are beautifully unique and gifted, just the way the Creator made you. His plans for you are beyond anything you could ever imagine, but you will never reach that destiny if you continue to conform to what the masses are doing. No one can be you and you can't be anyone else. And when you get dissatisfied with who you are and try to become a cheap copy of someone else, you're robbing the world of your gifting. And you're robbing yourself of the joy and power you could have if you lived with authenticity.

It took me a long time to finally get comfortable with how God made me. I'm not refined. I'm not an expert. Let's just say it—I'm a bit rough around the edges. I always wanted to be the whole package. You know what I'm talking about? That mom who always knows what to say at cocktail parties, instead of sticking an olive up her nose to see if she can shoot it across the room and hit someone in the back of the head.

One day, I was praying that God would change me. Then, I heard His voice speak to me. He said, "I didn't make a mistake, Hannah. You are how I made you and I made you that way for a reason. If you keep trying to be something you're not, you're going to rob yourself and the rest of the world of what I created you to be."

I was in tears. I didn't see how God could ever use a clown like me. But it was an act of faith to tear up the masks I tried to wear and exchange my plans for His, even if I didn't have any idea what His plans were.

Sometimes we think things can only be done one certain way and we try to conform to fit that blueprint. God is not only the author of our faith, but He is the finisher as well. He would never create you the way He created you if He did not have an extraordinary plan on how to use you for a great and mighty purpose.

I'm a Stallion, Baby!
There's one part of Shrek 2 where Donkey and Shrek both drink the "Happily Ever After" potion. Shrek turns into a drop-dead handsome guy; and Donkey turns into a white stallion. When Shrek is looking for Donkey, he asks a bunch of girls, "Have you seen my donkey?"

That's when Donkey prances all around and says, "I'm a stallion, baby!" He was so excited to finally be a stallion! To be respected and revered, no longer looked down upon. However, at the end of the movie, the potion's effects wore off and Donkey hung his head in despair. That's when Shrek pipes ups and says, "You still look like a noble steed to me."

How often do we get stuck in this mind frame where we need to look a certain way, or walk or talk like someone else in order to be who we want to be? I'll never have Kardashian boobs. I'll never have Jillian abs. It just ain't gonna happen. There is no plastic surgery that exists that can perform those kinds of miracles. Okay, maybe the boob part. But the point is that so many times our desperation to fit in and be accepted overrides our desperation to fulfill God's anointing over us. He has made you just the way He wants you. He sees the noble steed inside the donkey! And if we insist that we can't be happy or content as we are right now, then there is a high likelihood we will miss out on what God needs us to be.

Trust me. I've been there and done that. If you try to force yourself into a mold that God never intended you to fit it will just lead to frustration and anxiety, and very little real results. Don't be a cheap copy when you can be a priceless original!

God has anointed you to do something amazing in this world. It is your purpose. And when you put God's will over your own, you want to go where He wants you to go. You want to do what He wants you to do. It is His power pouring through you, and nothing you need to strain over. Sure it's effort, but it's good, energizing, fulfilling effort—just like moving around in your own skin. It takes all the pressure off! If you try to work outside of your anointing it becomes just that—work. That's what the Bible calls "toil." And God is very clear about pointing out that He never intended us to toil. He intended to do the work *through* us. What a relief!

"Unless the Lord builds the house, those who build it labor in vain. Unless the Lord watches over the city, the watchman stays awake in vain. It is in vain that you rise up early and go late to rest, eating the bread of anxious toil; for he gives to his beloved sleep." Psalm 127:1,2

Check it out. You can strive and toil all day long, but unless God is behind it, you will be eating the bread of anxious toil. Do you feel like you're stressed out and overworked? Maybe you need to step back and reevaluate for a minute. God never designed us for stress and toil. He designed us for peace and fruitfulness. When you are obedient to God and not trying to conform to the masses, there is an anointing on your life that makes everything seem easier.

"Anointing" means that His Spirit is working through you. It comes from ancient times when kings were anointed by priests with oil. It symbolized the power and presence of God working through a person. And it's the same with us today. Only now we live in a new covenant. Now, through the death and resurrection of Jesus Christ, we can actually have the Holy Spirit living within us. This often means saying "no" to your plans and "yes" to God's. But, wherever God leads you, He will not only provide for you, but He will give you the internal blessings of peace and joy that go along with His plans for your life. He created you for a purpose, and it's not to push and prod yourself into someone else's mold. He created you to be you—nothing less and nothing more.

God Uses Oddballs
Have you ever thought you just weren't good enough? You don't have the right education or family upbringing? Well, the truth of the matter is that God loves to use oddballs—

"God selected (deliberately chose) what in the world is foolish to put the wise to shame and what the world calls weak to put the strong to shame" (I Corinthians, 1:27).

Did you get a load of that? God has created you, imperfections and all, with the intent to pour His power through your weakness. He doesn't need any high-falutin' stallions prancing around. Lord knows, there are enough of those in the world. He wants YOU, just the way you are. Don't conform. Everyone does that. Be bold enough to be authentic and do your own thing, even if it seems a bit foolish to everyone else.

When you are your truest self, then you become moldable. God can then exalt you in your humility to be used for His greatness. Our weakness allows His strength to pour through us. Our foolishness allows His wisdom to go to work. He designed it that way on purpose so He would get the glory. And He deliberately chose you for the task, not when you clean up your mess or straighten yourself out or become the pro. Right now, exactly the way you are—mess and all. What freedom! God uses the obscure, the weird, the oddballs of the world so He can be God and show up in their lives. And if we're going to be honest here, we're all pretty quirky in our own distinct way.

I once heard someone say that it's not so much about finding your voice. It's about having the courage to use it. You don't need to set out on a path of self-discovery. Just think back to when you were a child. What were you like before you began to feel the pressure to conform? Where do you find your most joy? What are you doing when you feel you are being your truest self? I loved starting food fights, and to this day I can seriously tear up a kitchen.

Refuse to conform any longer. The longer you try to conform, the longer you are denying the world of your unique gifting, and the longer you are denying yourself of the abundant, extravagant life that God has designed you to live. He has your "happily ever after" all ready for you to walk into. No potion required.

Different Dreams, Different People
If you have more than one child, then you know all too well how two children, from the exact same mom and dad, can be dramatically different. Two of my boys are polar opposites—one is burly and blonde and as pale as the moon. The other is lean, brunette, and always seems to be sporting a tropical tan, even in the dead of winter. My oldest sister is still convinced that the blonde one must be a result of some torrid affair with a Swedish ski instructor that I've kept hidden. She even calls him Swen. (Sorry, not possible. I've only had one man my entire life—my husband, Blair. And he doesn't have a bit of Swede in him).

But it is truly remarkable how vastly different all seven of my kids are, even down to their pregnancies. With my oldest one, I was as big as a barn, topping the charts around 198 pounds! With my seventh kid, I only gained about seventeen pounds and looked like a stick with a basketball stuck under her shirt. With one of my girls, I was in labor for a good twenty-seven hours until she came out. It was absolutely miserable! With one of my sons, delivery was a breeze. I only had the chance to push through about two contractions before he came rushing in to the world. The doctor made it just in time to catch him. I remember we were watching "America's Funniest Home Videos" and I was laughing in between contractions!

Just as our kids are radically different, so are we. Even though we have the same heavenly Father, he has planted totally different dreams and desires within our spirits. Sometimes, giving birth to those dreams is a breeze. It seems as natural as leaves blowing in the breeze. But then other times, is seems we are stuck in the labor process. We push through, and push through, and it seems the dream just gets farther and farther away. I remember one of the nurses talking to me while I was in my hardest labor.

"Sweetie, she said. "You just have to relax. The more you tense up, the longer and harder it will be. You have to let your body do what your body is trying to do."

I wanted to give her a roundhouse kick to the face; but, I knew she was right. The more I tried to force something, the harder I was making it on myself. I was going for a natural childbirth, even if it meant I was kicking and screaming my way there. It was only when I relaxed completely, that the labor process sped up and I was able to hold my precious baby in my arms (thank you, epidural).

God is trying to do something miraculous through you. The more you try to conform to the world's method of doing things and insist on things going your way, the longer and harder you make it on yourself to give birth to those dreams that God planted inside of you. Relax. Be yourself. Let go of what you think you need to do and who you think you need to be; and trust in the One who knows you best.

God's Way, Not Yours
Just because God did something for one person doesn't mean He's committed to doing it for you. And just because He showed up in one way for someone, doesn't mean He's got to show up the same way for you as well. God cannot and will not be categorized. Think about all the different ways Jesus healed people. He tells a lame person to get up and walk. He touches another to heal their illness. He sends one person to go take a bath. He spits on dirt and rubs mud on a blind person's eyes. Some of His healings were immediate, while some took days to occur. For some healings, He wasn't even present. He just sent word by someone else. Jesus was unpredictable, to be sure. And God works the same way with us.

Even spiritual things can get stuck in the world of conformity. When John the Baptist came along, he was living out in the wilderness, eating locusts and honey, and cursing out all the super religious folks. Then Jesus came along and he spent his days hanging out with sinners, performing miracles, and going to parties. Both were on a mission and both did it radically different ways. Same heart, different hands.

Don't get stuck into thinking that one way is the only way. Sure, Jesus is the only way to the Father and apart from Him we can do nothing. But He shows his face in such radically different ways. He works just as much through a street preacher who is calling people to repent as He does through a billionaire CEO with a heart for God. Satan knows that if he can get the body of Christ turning on itself, then he can weaken our testimony. Don't judge others and don't copy them either. The most courageous thing you can do is to be the person God created you to be. Whether you realize it or not, you have a ministry. God has placed you where you are with the abilities you have for a reason.

It often happens that we get to know someone who is godly and prays four hours a day, so all of a sudden we think we're not holy enough if we don't pray four hours a day. If I tried to pray four hours a day, I'm pretty sure my brain would explode. God did not create me to hang out with him like that. I remember one time, I had a mentor who could pray and set the church on fire. She would rebuke demons left and right, and toss out some Old Testament names that I would make a note to myself to look up after prayer time was over. Her voice would practically shake the rafters and I'm pretty sure she sent the devil running for his life.

    I tried to pray like that. I felt that I wasn't spiritual enough because it didn't come naturally to me. I finally realized that the reason it didn't come out as natural was because it wasn't natural, not a bit. That wasn't how God created me, either. My time with God is more like, "Hey, God, look! It's a squirrel! Pretty!" Okay, maybe it's not that bad. But, what I'm trying to get you to understand is that God is amazingly unique and He creates us the same way. Just because God works some way with one of your friends doesn't mean He's that way with you.

    Don't try to pigeonhole God. He has something incredible for you, and only for you. Your miracle is coming. Maybe not in the way that Suzy or Bob got their miracle, but it's coming just the same. Don't get frustrated. Don't get jealous. Those emotions can quickly pull you out of your anointing and you'll be more miserable than ever. Just relax and know that He's working behind the scenes, preparing for your big moment.

    Let God be God and quit trying to predict His next move. So often we make our list of the potential breakthroughs that God can make on our behalf and then present it to Him like we're running a booth at the carnival ("Okay, God, pick a breakthrough, any breakthrough. I already did the hard work for you by coming up with all the options"). God doesn't need our options. He's already plotted out breakthroughs for you before you were even born, breakthroughs that would blow your mind.

    Let go. Relax. God doesn't need your help and He doesn't need your options. He just needs you—100% authentic you. The closer you get to Him; the less you think you have to figure everything out. Get to know Him better and better every day and He will move mountains on your behalf.

Middle School Mentality
God does not have an "in" crowd that He hangs with. The kingdom of God is not like middle school where every single girl looks exactly the same and they're all wearing the same labels. God loves variety. He adores different. God doesn't change; but He sure loves to show up in unique ways in unique people.

It's brutal in middle school if you don't conform. Show up with a Walmart shirt, and you could easily be banned for life (or at least by the yearbook committee). If you're going to live a radical life, you can't expect a lot of warm fuzzies to come from the rest of the crowd.

Refusing to conform isn't always easy. It's tough to go against the grain. And not everyone is going to support you in your decisions. We are called to live holy lives; and that often means making decisions that rub people the wrong way. It could be refusing to participate in a certain conversation that all your friends are having or driving the old beater car because you don't believe in taking out a loan. Or perhaps it means not letting your kids go see a movie that all the other kids are seeing or being the only mom who isn't griping about her husband at the playgroup meeting. Don't think that anyone is going to roll out the red carpet for you to live a different life from the one the masses choose. You already know that the gate is narrow and the pathway is constricted. You're going to have to suck it up and keep going.

You may not even find rallying support through the church. No one has a problem with people who go to church. It's when they start getting serious about all that God stuff that people start raising eyebrows.

I'm going to throw you a bone, here. If you're pleasing everyone around you, that's a big signal that you are conforming. When you choose the narrow pathway of nonconformity, you'll step on toes. No doubt about it. But, hold your peace. Hold your joy. There's no need to get your feathers all ruffled up over it. Just keep on keeping on.

God has great and mighty plans for you! You can either hang out in middle school where everyone just sinks in to conformity, or you can choose to live with boldness. You can be different. You can get radical and decide to live out your destiny. Don't rob the world of the gift of you. We need you, the real you.

For the longest time in my career, I tried to figure out what I could do to make money. I tried several pursuits, and they all fizzled and burned out (usually leaving me with a financial debt and a whole lot of discouragement). I finally decided to stop trying to make money and start doing what I love. I figured out that my greatest love was studying God's word, talking about His love, and being a mom. If I had all the money in the world and had the luxury to do whatever I wanted to do, that was what I would spend my time doing. So, I decided to just pretend like I was loaded and just do that thing that brought me joy. It was a radical decision because we were really struggling with money. But it wasn't until I freed myself of the shackles of conformity and just decided to be me, that things truly began to turn around in my life.

Are you ready for radical? Are you willing to go extreme? Our culture demands conformity. So, if you want to be blessed like crazy you've got to be willing to live like crazy and go against the tide. Let the rest of the crowd get suckered up into conformity. You are required to be one thing—yourself.

When the children of Israel were at the brink of the Promised Land, Moses sent twelve scouts to go check out the territory. Ten of them came back and said that there was no way they could defeat the giants who lived there. They said, "in our eyes we were like grasshoppers, and so we were in their eyes." But two men had a different perspective.—

"Caleb quieted the people before Moses, and said, Let us go up at once and possess it; we are well able to conquer it." Numbers 13:30

Basically, Joshua and Caleb said, "We can take them. Let's go!" So, do you think the majority changed their mind? Do you think they agreed with Joshua and Caleb, put on their armor, and grabbed their swords? No way! In fact, the majority got so mad at Joshua and Caleb, the nonconformists, they threatened to kill them. When you have the guts to stand out and be different, don't expect the world to run and embrace you. If you carry your cross, expect to be crucified to it. Sometimes it hurts to be different, but I'd rather feel the hurt of authenticity and pay the price of conformity.

But, here's the good news. Out of all twelve spies, only two of them ever entered the Promised Land. You got it—Joshua and Caleb.

You're on the brink of your Promised Land. You are right on the edge of a miracle. I can feel it. Even as I'm writing this right now, God is pulling the words out of me to make their way to you. At the same time, that promise He has placed in you is rising up to come forward. He's pulling the promise out of you. You have been led to this moment, at this time, to witness something miraculous. Promise and confirmation, uniting with such power and glory that the Spirit of God becomes tangible. You can feel it. He is speaking to your heart right now, saying, "I love you just the way you are. Be who I created you to be—nothing more, nothing less. Let go and witness what I can do through your life. My precious child, it's time. Step into your promise."

There is power in surrendering to your truest self. The next move is up to you. Are you going to have the guts to be different? The boldness to break out of the masses? It's time to leave behind that middle school mentality, and believe for something greater. I declare it right now that you are digging in your heels and no longer conforming to the masses. Beginning right now, you are living your truest self. You are becoming the person that God designed you to be. And this time you're going to own it!

www.hannahhelpme.com

CRAZY BONUS!
Are you living your truest self?
Check out the FREE video, "One and Only" and find out!
Click on the link RIGHT HERE, or go to
www.hannahkeeley.com/blog/trueself.

STEP 6
DROP THE DEAD WEIGHT

I'm a tightwad. Always have been; always will be. I remember one time I was looking out the window, watching my kids play ball. I saw my son take two bites out of an apple before he threw it into the woods so he could step up to bat. I went out there and made him find the apple, rinse it off, and eat the rest of it. Yes, it's a true story and he will be more than happy to verify it. I don't waste anything!

So, knowing my philosophy on saving money, you'll understand why I did what I did on this particular autumn day back in 2010. We were enjoying a wonderful family vacation in Florida; and had decided to spend the entire day at Universal Studios. We ate breakfast at the hotel and got to Universal Studios early to enjoy a day of fun with the family. Now, I love roller coasters, so that was our very first stop. I didn't even consider the egg and spinach omelet I had eaten right before riding the Dueling Dragons—twice! When I got off, I felt like my stomach was still on that third turn with the spiral twist. I tried to shake it off, but just couldn't.

Then it hit. I knew that omelet was no longer going to be satisfied to stay in my stomach. I had to find a toilet, fast! I felt like I was in some action spy movie—I scoped out the closest bathroom and headed there as fast as I could, knowing I had only seconds to go before the bomb went off. The vomit was coming up and puke was eminent. I took off my jacket and held it in front of my face, just in case I didn't make it to the bathroom.

I didn't make it to the bathroom.

I was about three yards away when the floodgates opened and omelet puke exploded out. And I'm not even kidding. It exploded. If my jacket had not been in front of my face, I'm pretty sure everyone within ten feet of me would have been baptized in vomit.

So, there I was, in the bathroom. I had finished throwing up and was trying to clean my self up, splashing water on my face and drying it off with brown paper towels. But I didn't know what to do about my jacket. The inside of it was covered in puke. Although it wasn't expensive (I had bought it at the thrift store), I didn't want to throw it away. After all, it was a good jacket. So, you see my dilemma, right?

I wiped off the inside as well as I could and then balled it all up, covered it in paper towels, and stuck it in a plastic bag. I then put the puke package inside my backpack and went back outside where my husband was waiting.

Being the perpetual gentleman, Blair reached for my backpack and put it on his shoulders to carry while we were at the park. The incident was over. I felt better. We could just continue on with a wonderful family vacation, and everything could go on swimmingly.

Until about three in the afternoon when the sun came out and warmed up the park—and the backpack.

Blair began complaining about some nasty odor he was smelling. He kept trying to walk away from it, but it was following him everywhere he went! I went through the typical family stink scenarios—someone forgot their deodorant? No. A dirty diaper? No. Maybe someone had stuck their stinky socks in the backpack…

Oh, wait. The backpack.

"Umm, Blair?" I said, as innocently as possible, "I think I know where that smell is coming from."

"Where?" he asked.

"I threw up all over my jacket and stuck it in the backpack," I confessed. Blair stopped dead in his tracks and looked at me incredulously.

"Are you serious?" he asked. "You saved that jacket?" He was evidently appalled at how far I was taking this whole tightwad thing. He immediately stripped off the backpack, pulled out the puke package with one hand while holding his nose with the other hand, and dumped the entire thing in the closest trashcan.

My jaw dropped.

"But, Blair," I protested. "I don't want to throw away a perfectly good jacket."

"Honey," he said, "there is nothing *perfect* or *good* about that jacket anymore. It's staying in the trash where it belongs!" Sometimes a man just has to put his foot down; and in this case, I knew Blair wasn't going to budge.

He put back on the backpack, lightened of both a heavy load and a noxious odor, and breathed a deep sigh of relief. I had given up a puke-covered jacket in return for a happy husband—not a bad trade at all.

What Are You Carrying Around?

I wonder sometimes how many of us are carrying stinky junk around in our backpacks. How many moms are letting their pasts destroy their future simply because we won't let go of the pain. God never intended for you to stay where you are. I firmly believe your best days are in front of you. But, you will never get to those best days if you don't let go of the pain that is holding you back. Remember how the path to life is narrow and constricted? There is no room on this path for the baggage of your past. It may seem bizarre, but the things we most desperately hold on to are usually the rotting, stinking, stuff that is destroying us anyway (festering, puke-covered jacket, anyone?)

I've heard it before from so many moms—"but I can't get past it!" I know it's hard to shut the door on your hurt. Perhaps it's a relationship that didn't work out, or a personal loss that still grips your soul, or even a career that fizzled and died. But you will never open the door to a better future until you can shut the door of a rotten past. You'll just be stuck in the doorway, kind of like those automatic doors at the grocery store. Until you can walk through the entrance where the muddy mats lie on the ground and the grocery carts are stacked by the wall, you can't get into the place where abundance spills out of every shelf and bin. God wants to take you shopping and He's willing to foot the bill. But you can't do it until you can move forward and let those doors shut behind you once and for all.

The enemy wants to rob you of your future. That's why he keeps the pain so fresh in your mind and keeps reminding you of the hurt you've had to endure. That's why he constantly whispers to you about all the people who have done you wrong, all the opportunities that slipped by, and all the mistakes you've made. He knows that if he can keep you stuck in the past, he will be able to rob you of the abundance that lies in your future.

If you have made mistakes in your past, you're not the only one. We've all sinned. That's why God's Word is such good news:

"If we [freely] admit that we have sinned and confess our sins, He is faithful and just (true to His own nature and promises) and will forgive our sins [dismiss our lawlessness] and [continuously] cleanse us from all unrighteousness [everything not in conformity to His will in purpose, thought, and action]." I John 1:9

Let me break it down for you: God wants a relationship with you. He wants a great life for you. It actually makes Him happy to make you happy. So when you screw up and get off-track, He always supplies a way to restore that relationship and make things right again. You can leave the past in the past and be free again. The problem is never God forgiving you; it's you forgiving yourself. Step back and see the battle for what it really is. God's not holding guilt over you. He has forgotten all about it. Satan is a master at using guilt; and he reminds you every chance he has.

Remember those horrible things you said to your child?
Remember that money you lost in that business scam?

Remember that pain? That divorce? That addictio

Satan is crafty and he can paint pictures of guilt in ou. minds, and replay our sins in painfully accurate detail in order to defeat us. When you feel that guilt whispering, and those scenarios being replayed, understand who is doing the whispering and call him out on it.

"No more, Satan. I'm forgiven! I'm free! God has forgiven my sins and He has cleansed me from all unrighteousness. So, take your lies back to hell where they belong!"

You've got to get serious when dealing with the devil. Whining about it doesn't work. Crying about it doesn't work. What works is when you take the affirmative. Use God's word because it's the only weapon you have. Take I John 1:9 and stick it right back in Satan's face. Memorize it and pull it out to slice the lie apart. Satan can't stand against the Word of God. When you wield that weapon, he's powerless.

Spiritual warfare is kind of like taking family road trips. The kids can be misbehaving in the back of the van and you can whine about it, complain about it, and even threaten the kids, but they know you mean business when you pull the van off to the side of the road and unbuckle your seatbelt.

It's time to pull off to the side of the road.

You've got to let Satan know you mean business and that only happens when you pull out the Word of God. Quit talking to your friends about your pain, quit thinking about your pain, quit griping to your family about your pain, and—yes, I know this may sound a bit extreme—but quit talking to God about how big your pain is. That's just rehashing the same old story. Instead, take the offensive, and start talking to your pain about how big your God is!

In the Stupid Business

Like many families with a lot of kids, we have been through some really lean years financially. I remember one time, when I had the idea to begin a baby products business to bring in more money. Well, I was suckered into the philosophy that it takes money to make money. Since I didn't have any money to invest in my brilliant idea, I decided to borrow it by taking out a loan against our home.

One thing led to another and before I knew it, we were $35,000 dollars in the hole, maxed out on our line of credit, and I had not even sold the first product. We finally decided to cut our losses and stop going in a direction that God had never given us in the first place.

Wow, oh, wow…the guilt hit hard! It was my idea to start a business, my choice to take out a loan, my mistake to borrow money for an idea that didn't even represent a sellable product. I could fill a book with all the things I did wrong!

Now we were more strapped than ever before and I had nothing to show for it except wasted years and lots of debt. I felt like I had let down my husband and my kids (that money could have paid for college!).

Finally, I confessed my sin to God and to my husband (and even to my kids). God forgave me. My family forgave me. But I just couldn't seem to move past it. Every time I paid bills, it was brought to mind. When I lied down at night, it stewed in my head. When we couldn't pay for something, it hit me in the pit of my stomach.

Then I dived into God's word and got a fresh wind of His mercy. He had forgiven me; I realized that. But what really got me excited was that He would restore me! Although we have to suffer for our sins, He promises that He will restore us if we stay faithful. That's when I took the offensive. I began paying off my bills knowing that God would restore my finances. I stopped brooding over the lost years because I knew that God would restore that time. He's the Creator of time and he packs our life full of living! God is faithful to restore you. You have to be faithful to leave the past behind.

The Hurt in Haran
Sometimes the hurt doesn't come from the guilt you carry around. Sometimes the hurt comes from a different place—a place you seem to have no control over. It's not something

wrong you did, but something wrong that was done to you. Maybe you're having a hard time forgiving someone who hurt you or robbed you. Perhaps you're even holding bitterness toward God for a loss that you had to suffer through. There is pain that won't go away and hurt that can't be healed. And sometimes you feel like you're the only one in the whole world who seems to be suffering.

You're not the only one.

Before God called Abraham to go to the Promised Land, He put that same dream in the heart of Abraham's father, Terah.

The story goes like this: Before Terah had Abraham, he had another son named Haran. He was his pride and joy, his firstborn son. As a firstborn son, he also had the coveted position of carrying on his father's name and receiving his inheritance and blessing. But things didn't really go as planned for Terah. And when things don't go as planned, there's usually a lot of hurt and pain that go along with it. Terah's firstborn son, Haran, died. His pride and joy, his inheritance, his firstborn son, died. With Haran's death, Terah's dream died as well. I couldn't imagine any greater hurt than the death of a child, and on top of that, the death of your inheritance.

But in the middle of this despair, God gave Terah a dream—to leave his hometown of Ur and head out to Canaan. Terah shook off his hurt, gathered up his goods, and set off on a journey. But on the way, he stopped in a town called, of all things, Haran. Could you imagine that? You set out to reach your dream, and the biggest hurt from your past raises its ugly head and reminds you, every minute, of the pain you still carry around. Every time you say the name of the town where you live, every time you write your address, every step you take outside your home, you're reminded of your son's death. You can't escape it. You can't shake it. No matter what you do, it's there to haunt you at every turn.

Terah had a choice. He could stay in Haran and wallow in his bitterness; or he could gather up his things and move on toward Canann, toward the dream God had placed in his heart.

Genesis 11:31 tells us "when they came to Haran, they settled there." The very next verse says something even more heartbreaking, "Terah died in Haran." I wonder how many of us settle in our sorrow instead of moving on to the greatness that God has in store. Pretty soon that settling leads to a rut, and that rut closes in to become a grave. I know it's hard to shake pain. Just when you feel like the sun is breaking, those storm clouds move in and the bitterness once again has your soul in a death grip.

But we can do something about it. We need to take off the sorrow at every turn and consciously put on the mantle of joy.

Nehemiah 8:10 says, "be not grieved and depressed, for the joy of the Lord is your strength and your stronghold." Satan is after your joy. He knows if he's got that, then he's got your strength. That's why he never wants those wounds from your past to heal. That's why he's always reminding us of the pain that we can't seem to shake. When we hold on to bitterness, we shut the door to blessings in our future. You can be bitter or you can be blessed, but you can't be both.

There is a time for grief and sadness. We can't experience a loss without experiencing the pain that goes along with it. But it is meant to last for a season. You were never meant to drag it behind you the rest of your life. Sorrow lasts for a night. Joy comes in the morning.

Today is the day. Your morning has broken! It's time to forgive the person who hurt you and free yourself from the prison of pain. It's time to forgive God, because He is the only One Who can help you through it. That rotting mess you're carrying around is dead, and it's robbing you of the life God wants you to live. Quit harboring bitterness and open ourselves up to the possibility of God doing something even greater than you could imagine. Whatever wrong you have done and whatever wrong has been done to you, now is the time to toss away the baggage and experience freedom.

If you feel stuck in your own Haran, then it's going to be a tough journey out. Satan will keep grabbing at you, trying to pull you back into pain. But it can happen; and it *will* happen if you consciously make the decision to shake it off and step out, day by day, moment by moment.

Restoration Hardware
"Restoration Hardware" is a lot more than the name of a store that makes all homeowners drool. It's God's method of making it all better. God wants to restore you. Through His Word, Almighty God has provided the hardware to make that happen. What an awesome God we serve! He does more than just heal the hurt. He pays you back!

God's word tells us that when a thief is found, he must make restitution for whatever he stole. Check it out!

"But if he is found out, he must restore seven times [what he stole]; he must give the whole substance of his house [if necessary—to meet his fine]." Proverbs 6:31

Satan is a thief. He is constantly trying to steal our joy, snatch away our faith, and rob us of our strength. And, guess what, he gets away with it every day!

It's time to discover the thief and catch him red-handed! Quit blaming people, the economy, the boss, your spouse, the kids. Truth is, the enemy is stalking around trying to use everything in his power to tear you down. Satan is the thief who has robbed you. It could be he has stolen your peace and joy, or maybe he has robbed you of years you spent in a bad relationship, money you worked hard for, or a childhood you never got to experience.

The loss is painful, but here's the good news. God doesn't just make it better. He has promised that when the thief is discovered, he will be required to provide restitution. God will make sure you get double, triple, or even seven times back for your trouble. Quit the blame game. There's only one person to blame and the best way to get back at the enemy is to stop the grumbling and hold on to your joy. Oh, that drives Satan crazy!

God's Word is your hardware. Sink down into it and ~~th~~e promises of restitution that are coming your way. When the bitterness starts to creep in, you are the only one who can overcome it. You already have authority over it. You just need to take action on it. When the enemy begins whispering those same scenarios, just strike back with God's Word.

Here's some hardware you can use:
- God, thank You that after I have suffered for awhile, You have promised to restore, confirm, strengthen, and establish me (I Peter 5:10).
- Thank You that the former things have all passed away and You make all things new (Rev. 21:4).
- Thank You that although I have seen many troubles, You have promised to revive me from the depths of the earth and bring me up again (Psalm 71:20).
- Thank You that You have given me beauty instead of ashes, the oil of gladness instead of mourning, and a garment of praise instead of a spirit of despair (Isaiah 61:3).

Remember, God can't pull you out of a pit if you prefer to wallow in it. You have to make a conscious decision to claim joy when you feel the bitterness come on and refuse to go back to that place of pain again. You need to step out in faith and say, "God is restoring to me everything I've got coming. Satan may have stolen from me, but God's going to pay me back—double, triple, even seven times over!"

Why We Want the Jacket

I remember talking to a friend on the phone one day. He was frustrated at a recent business loss. He had gone into a business venture with a friend. It looked like a great investment and his friend eventually convinced him to put his entire life savings into the business. Then, in a matter of two years, the entire business went belly-up. His entire investment, his life savings, his kids' college fund, everything he had squandered and saved for decades, was gone in less than 24 months. And the worst part of it all was that after the business was a wash-out, his friend seemed to drop off the face of the earth, without so much as an apology or any attempt to right the wrong. Now, that's a fine "how do you do," isn't it?

As you can imagine, his pain was deep. Not only did he feel the hurt of losing all his savings, but he also felt the sting of betrayal. And the enemy made sure he wasn't getting past it. One day, his wife couldn't get in her car because the door was stuck. After laboring over it for hours, my friend was eventually able to repair it with some duct tape and a wire coat hanger. But the trick was, she could get in, but she couldn't get out. Whenever she wanted to get out of the car, she had to slide over and use the passenger door. He called me with bitterness dripping off his words.

"I'm just so sick over it!" he complained. "All because I lost every penny in that stupid scheme, my wife has to drive around in a tin can with the door jerry-rigged. I just can't let it go. The regret follows me around all day and keeps me up all night."

"Every day you keep carrying around this bitterness, you're digging a grave that is getting harder and harder to climb out of," I said.

"I know, but I just can't let it go," he said. I listened to him go on and on, complaining about his finances. Then I finally broke in.

"Do you like dog puke?" I asked him. There was a strange silence on the other line.

"No, not particularly," he mumbled. "Why?"

"Because you keep going back to it over and over again," I told him.

Proverbs 26:11 tells us that "As a dog returns to his vomit, so a fool returns to his folly." It's foolish to think that dwelling on a painful past will do anything to heal the hurt. On the contrary, you're just playing right into Satan's hands. He's got you right where he wants you, bitter and blaming. Quit returning to that same pain and hurt over and over again. It's time to forgive, move on, and experience freedom. Don't keep going back to the dog puke, or omelet puke, or whatever your puke of choice may be. No matter what you want to call it, it's nothing but vomit. And the longer you carry it around, the heavier and stinkier the load becomes. It's time to toss it off and trust God that He is going to restore you, better than you were before!

But we keep holding on. We keep going back to that same dull pain. One reason we hold on is because, as stinky and burdensome as the bitterness is, it is a shield from our own greatness. Most of the time, it's not our failures that haunt us; it's the reality of our greatness that shakes us to the bones.

God said in His Word that His plans for us are immeasurably more than we can ask or think or imagine (Ephesians 3:20). He told us that all authority on heaven and earth has been given to us. He told us that we will do even greater things than He did because the Holy Spirit was with us:

"I assure you, most solemnly I tell you, if anyone steadfastly believes in Me, he will himself be able to do the things that I do; and he will do even greater things than these, because I go to the Father." John 14:12

That's right. It's not a typo—greater things than the Man who healed the sick, raised the dead, walked on water, turned scraps into a feast, and changed the world! If that doesn't send you for a loop, then I don't know what will!

God is not a man that He would lie, so then the reality hits—*I was born for greatness*. But our spiritual reality and our physical reality doesn't quite synch up. 'If I was born for greatness,' you may be thinking, 'then why is my life turning out so bad?' The reality is we carry a blessing from God. It covers us from head to toe and it is that power that enables us to live out this greatness that God's word describes. Although we were created for greatness, we were born into a cursed world. If we're not careful, that curse can put layer upon layer over our greatness, each layer hiding more of God's glorious light.

Remember what it was like to be a little kid? You could do anything and be anything! There were no limits in your imagination. God looked down at His people carrying around His glorious blessing and said, "Now nothing they imagine will be impossible for them" (Genesis 11:6) It's true! He planted dreams and desires in us because that is His intention for us—to live big, bold, lives with impact.

But hurt happens. Pain happens. It could be abuse you suffered through, bad relationships, hurtful words, dreams that fizzled and died, humiliation, despair, grief. The curse has its toll on our lives and the baggage starts piling up. Pretty soon, our glorious intention doesn't even have a glimmer left. And as crazy as it sounds, we choose the baggage. We hold on to the hurt. We cling to that vomit-soaked jacket *because it's the only thing we know!* It's the only thing that stands in the way between us and the gut-wrenching reality that God intended us for greatness.

It becomes our excuse, a crutch we can lean on in order to have an "out" from the real game that God created us to play. We choose to hang out in the corner watching the super achievers from a distance, all the time convincing ourselves of the lie that some people were destined for greatness and some people weren't.

Here's the truth. When you accept Jesus Christ as your Savior, you automatically have that blessing. You have the Spirit of the Living God dwelling inside of you. God is not partial. He doesn't play favorites. He gives His Spirit to all people who claim Him as Lord—not a little or a lot, but His *whole* and *complete* Spirit. Just think—the very presence of the Most High God, the Creator of the heavens and the earth, is living inside of you right now! You can cover it in a cloak of despair and bitterness. Or you can choose to take off the baggage and finally live out your greatness.

Time to Let It Go

A few months ago, I was driving down the road in my 15-passenger van (I totally rule the road in that sucker), and I veered over a bit into the other lane when I was turning the corner. Just for the record, it's kind of hard not to, okay?

Anyway, the car to my left honked his horn, and when I looked over (or I should say, "down and over" since I was about twelve feet off the ground) I noticed that he was struggling to hold on to the wheel with his left hand while he stretched across the entire length of the front seat in order to flip me off with his right hand. It was hysterical. Since I was so high up off the ground in the van, it made flipping me off totally impractical for him. I wouldn't be able to see him properly. Therefore, he was practically stretching into a yoga pose so he could make sure I saw his obscene gesture out the window on the passenger side.

So I smiled and waved.

It's really not so hard to forgive people when you realize that we are all flawed in some way. Some people are walking around in so much pain you couldn't even imagine what they are suffering through. And hurting people have a tendency to hurt people. You never know what people are going through. Faces hide a lot; and you may be the only mercy they have ever come across in a very long time.

And then there are some people who are just stupid. Yeah, I said it. There are some foolish people out there who truly don't even know better. We've all taken stupid pills on occasion, so be merciful toward others and quick to forgive. Lord knows, I've been mean, hurtful, stupid, arrogant, and sometimes all of that in a five-minute time span. We've all made mistakes. But God has mercy toward us, so we can extend that same mercy toward others.

Forgiven and Set Free

Let the baggage go. You can't move further along in your life until you can free yourself of the past. In fact, I don't even want you to go further along in this book until you can let go of the pain. The bitterness and despair will constantly be those shackles around your ankles, preventing you from running in God's power.

Honestly, none of us deserve God's grace and that's what's so amazing about it. He forgives us every time we ask Him to. His mercy is new to us every morning. It never stops. No matter what the sin, His grace covers it.

That's why Jesus died. He died as a sacrifice to break the curse of our separation from God. He died so we could have God's glorious presence living within us. When Jesus hung on the cross and said, "It is finished." He sealed it. We don't need to add anything to the gift He's already given us. It's not what we do that gets us to God or what we say that earns us brownie points in heaven. It's Jesus.

When you catch a glimpse of God's grace and mercy, you can let go of the pain from your past. All that abuse? It is finished. All that hurt? It is finished. The bitterness? The jealousy? The anger? The resentment? The self-loathing? It is all finished! You are a new creation in Christ and His power lives within you.

Because of God's mercy, you can extend mercy. You are not the one forgiving the people who hurt you. It is God's mercy pouring through you. And just like His mercy is new every morning, we need to extend that same mercy every morning. Start each morning off without the baggage. Say it out loud if you need to—"I am forgiven! And I have forgiven those who have hurt me. I have let them go. I am free to love like God loves. I am blessed and I bless others."

Keep stepping out in mercy, day by day, and you will find that those layers of bitterness come off, one at a time, until that glorious light begins to glow brighter and brighter in you. It is truly a miraculous thing when you step out of the dark and into the greatness that God created you to live.

So, open that backpack, pull out that puke-covered jacket, and toss it in the garbage where it belongs. You are free! You were destined for greatness! I declare it over you right now. In the name of Jesus Christ, you are free. Because of His love that pours through you, you are able to love the unlovable and to have mercy on the unmerciful. The shackles around your ankles are broken and destroyed, and you are free to run in God's grace.

www.hannahhelpme.com

The dead and rotting bones from your past are buried forever and in their place are resurrected dreams and visions that have been abandoned. You are free to assume your rightful position as one of the blessed, one of the favored, one who carries around the Spirit of the All Powerful God. You are released from your pain and free to pursue your promised land. You are free to imagine and create. You are free!

CRAZY BONUS!
Are you carrying around some junk in your trunk?
Check out this video and find out now!
Click on the link <u>RIGHT HERE</u>, or visit
www.hannahkeeley.com/blog/junk

STEP 7
SPARK YOUR SUPER POWERS

My three sons are sandwiched right in between two pairs of girls—two older sisters that love to boss them around and two younger sisters that love to boss them around. Fortunately, they're superheroes; so they can take the pressure. When they were younger, they would constantly play together in our woods—scaling trees, running at super speed, lifting cars. Their talents knew no end.

Eventually, they settled in to their own characters. My oldest son, Kyler, became Mighty Man; while my middle son, Karis became Rubber Boy. As you can probably deduce, Mighty Man had super strength while Rubber Boy could stretch to incredible lengths. Then it came time for my youngest son to choose his character.

They were outside playing superheroes when Korben streaked inside, his face rosy and glowing from running with his older brothers through the woods. His shoes were caked with dirt, and his caramel-colored hair stuck to his face with sweat. He came running up to me in the living room where I was folding clothes, and looked up into my face.

"I want to be five," he said.

"You are five." I told him.

"No, that's my superhero name," he explained.

I thought for a while....Nope, nowhere in my exhaustive knowledge and experience in the area of parenting could I find any reference point for understanding this concept that Korben was now proposing.

"You want your superhero name to be a number?" I asked him, slowly.

"Yeah!" he answered enthusiastically.

I thought maybe he didn't understand the whole idea of superhero identities so I began to explain it to him.

"You know how Kyler is Mighty Man and he has mighty strength?" I asked.

"Uh huh," Korben answered.

"And Karis is called Rubber Boy because he's really stretchy." I said.

"Uh huh," he said, looking at me with those blue eyes as big as saucers.

"Usually Superheroes take a name that's kind of like what they do," I said. "Spiderman can shoot webs like a spider. The Human Torch can light up into fire. And the Hulk is this big, massive, strong dude," I continued.

"I just like five," he answered.

"You mean you like being five years old?" I asked.

"No, that's my superhero name," he replied.

I could see I was getting nowhere. It's called a circular argument. You eventually learn to do this type of arguing really well, especially when your kids get to be teenagers.

"Well, what is your superhero talent?" I asked. "What can you do?"

He didn't even hesitate in responding, "Everything!" he said.

The next day, I drove to the fabric store to buy some brightly-colored cloth and some iron-on backing. When I got home, I created their superhero costumes. After all, every superhero needs a costume, right? Kyler had a blue shirt with a big red "M" on the front. Karis had a red shirt with a big blue "R." And Korben's shirt was yellow with a big, green number 5 on the front. It wasn't spandex, but it would do. As soon as those shirts got out of the wash, they were on their bodies. I think I eventually cut corners and just decided not to launder them anymore. Little boy body odor is no big deal, especially when you live in a home with nine people and there are so many other smells to compete with!

They eventually became a common site the neighborhood. Who were those three boys with the weird homemade shirts? Is it a bird? Is it a plane? No way! It's the dynamic trio—M, R, and 5 (not to be confused with 4 or 6).

You're a Superhero

I'm sure most of us wish we had super powers. It would be so cool if we could clone ourselves for just a few days. One of us could watch the kids while the other painted the bedroom. Or if we could become invisible! Wouldn't that come in handy when parenting teens? Or how about if we could grow knives out of our knuckles like Wolverine? That would be epic! Not really that useful, unless you're cutting up vegetables for soup, but epic just the same!

The good news is that we have access to super powers that would totally blow you away! You know how Superman can leap over tall buildings? How the Hulk can crash through walls? That's nothing. Check this out:

"For by You I can run through a troop, and by my God I can leap over a wall." Psalm 18:29

Running through a troop? Leaping over walls? Wowzers! I think most of us would be happy if we could just get our families around the dinner table and match a pair of socks! But, God's power is more amazing and awesome than we can even understand. And the coolest thing of all is that as believers, we have total access to it! The only problem is that very few of us actually take advantage of it. It's kind of like Tony Stark having this awesome crime-fighting suit, but never stepping into it. There would be no Ironman! Super Powers aren't just for the pages of a Marvel comic book. The Bible talks about super powers that come straight from God:

"But you shall receive power (ability, efficiency, and might) when the Holy Spirit has come upon you, and you shall be My witnesses in Jerusalem and all Judea and Samaria and to the ends (the very bounds) of the earth." Acts 1:8

In this verse, Jesus was talking to His disciples, instructing them to wait for the Holy Spirit so they would have the power to be witnesses and share Jesus with people all over the earth. But, you don't have to be serving as a missionary to be a witness. At your job, you are a witness to your co-workers. In your home, you are a witness to your children. In your marriage, you are a witness to your spouse. You don't have to dig a well in Zimbabwe or build a house in Bangladesh. God has placed you right where you are with a specific purpose. And every one of us, if we are believers in Christ, have the responsibility to share His message with the people He has placed in our lives and to live out His message in the tasks He has placed before us. I believe this verse is speaking to every single one of us. He has a glorious purpose for each of us, but it is only through the power of the Holy Spirit that we can fulfill it.

Acts 1:8 is a wonderful promise. It tells us that we will receive power—ability, efficiency, and might. This sounds like a recipe for a superhero if I ever heard one. I can't think of a single person out there who could not use a little more ability, efficiency, and might. But like I said, it's only through the power of the Holy Spirit. The Holy Spirit needs to be living in you. This means God has to be in first place and you need to be living within the standards and the boundaries that God set for you. You can't walk around yelling at your kids and griping at your husband and expect God's power to pour through you. It just doesn't work that way. God wants to empower you, but you've got to clear the gunk out of your life and make room.

As you take measures to live a life that is pleasing to God, He begins to pour super powers in you. Now, I know it can be difficult to change a lifetime of habits, especially if they are negative ones. Fortunately, God understands this.

"But He said to me, My grace (My favor and loving-kindness and mercy) is enough for you [sufficient against any danger and enables you to bear the trouble manfully]; for My strength and power are made perfect (fulfilled and completed) and show themselves most effective in [your] weakness. Therefore, I will all the more gladly glory in my weaknesses and infirmities, that the strength and power of Christ (the Messiah) may rest (yes, may pitch a tent over and dwell) upon me!" 2 Corinthians 12:9

Remember, Grace is "undeserved favor." He gives us favor, loving-kindness, and mercy, not because we deserve it but because He loves us. He is on our side, cheering us on, encouraging us, and enabling us to live lives that please Him. And when we begin to show God's character through our own lives, then we begin to show supernatural powers as well—abilities we never thought we would ever possess, efficiency to get more done in less time, and might to keep going even during the tough times. It is not something we could ever do on our own. It is totally an act of God.

Even though we don't know how we are ever going to change, God can take those weak places in our lives and in our personalities and pour His healing and wholeness into them. But we've got to be willing to change.

One time a friend was complaining to me about her relationship with her boyfriend. They just couldn't seem to work things out and were always fighting. She wanted me to pray for them. Usually, that would be just fine; but I also knew this person very well. She had suffered through two previous broken relationships, and had been sexually active in both of them. Now, she and her current boyfriend were living together (and sleeping together) and were fighting all the time.

I told her that God really wants wholeness and happiness in her life, but as long as she was living outside of the boundaries that He set for her, it wasn't going to work out. *God is not going to enable and empower you to live in disobedience to Him.* It is important to understand this, because way too many people go through their lives wondering why God isn't stepping in to rescue them when they are sinking in the consequences of their own poor choices. People want their cake and eat it, too. Stretching out of our comfort zones and changing our lives in order to live by God's standards is never going to feel good. But do you want to be comfortable? Or do you want to be powerful? Because there is a world of difference between the two! You can stay comfortable (and, yes, people are even comfortable living in crap) and miss out on God's blessings for your life. Or you can get uncomfortable, shake off your excuses, and step into the glorious, abundant life that God wants for you.

Tough Lesson
I had to learn this lesson of disobedience the hard way. One summer, we were really strapped for money. When Blair would bring home his paycheck, I would wait until all the bills were paid to see if we had enough money leftover for our tithe. Deep inside, I knew this was wrong. God does not want our leftovers. He commands that we bring Him the "first fruits."

I knew this, good and well, but continued in disobedience. In my human mind, I didn't know how I was going to afford groceries and keep the electricity on in the house. I wasn't taking God at His promise that He would supply all my needs. After several weeks, Blair's car broke down and we had to get the fuel pump replaced. Two weeks after that, my tire blew out and I had to get a new set. Then a month after that, I took Blair's car to the grocery store and when I came out I saw a note stuck under my wind shield. It said, "I would hate to see the owner of this car have a blow out on the highway. Please get these tires replaced for your own safety." I looked down and could see that the treads had worn entirely down. I began praying and asking God, "Why are you doing this?" Then I felt God tell me, "Why are you not trusting me?" Here I was, living in disobedience, expecting God to empower me.

I was trying to scrape by instead of trusting God to empower me to live in a way that glorifies and honors Him. Not only was I disobeying God, but I was also preventing myself from living a greater, more fulfilling life. I was cutting off my power supply!

I certainly learned a lot that summer. God's power is unlimited. He will give you the strength, energy, time, resources (yes, that includes money) to do everything He has commanded you to do. When we disobey Him, it's like cutting off that power supply. After a new fuel pump, and two new sets of tires, I realized that the money was God's and not my own. When I began tithing the first fruits, He multiplied the 90% left over to make it go further than the 100% I had to begin with. That's just one of the miraculous ways God's power works!

Our Weakness, God's Strength
We all disobey God and do stupid stuff. And if I live to be 200 years old, I will still be doing stupid stuff, although I am getting better. Praise God! In Romans 3:23, it says we all have sinned and we all fall short of the glory of God. You sin, I sin, we all sin. Fortunately, God sent His son, Jesus to pay the price for all that sin. Praise the Lord! God's grace covers our sin. But, we can be a believer and still live a miserable life if we continue doing stupid stuff, even when we know better. God wants you to go to heaven, but He also wants you to live a productive, fulfilling, super power-filled life while you're here on earth. That happens when we live in obedience to God and never stop striving to do what is right.

"What shall we say [to all this]? Are we to remain in sin in order that God's grace (favor and mercy) may multiply and overflow? Certainly not! How can we who died to sin live in it any longer?" Romans 6:1-2

God is never going to force you to live righteously. But He really, really wants you to—not for Him, but for you! When you live righteously, always growing in God and trying to live in a way that pleases Him, you open up the door for God's blessings to pour into your life. And what a great life it is!

2 Corinthians 12:9, it also states that God's power is most effectively shown through our weaknesses. How cool is it that we don't have to get dropped in a vat of toxic waste or get bitten by a radioactive spider in order to get super powers? With God, it is not our strength that enables us to get super powers, but our weaknesses! God tells us in this passage that when we are weak, He will be strong. If we could be awesome in our own strength, then we wouldn't need God, would we? But we all have weaknesses.

It's okay to have weak areas in your life. Maybe you are inclined to anger, envy, or gossip. Perhaps you hold on to bitterness or worry. It could even be that you are not diligent with the blessings God has given you. We all have weak areas. It's okay to have them; but it's not okay to allow them to control you. We need to confess our weaknesses to God and then discipline ourselves to get them under control. And we can, with God's help.

For the longest time, I was a horrible procrastinator. I would waste time thinking about ways to waste time. I also have an attention span that is microscopic in size. I would often pass off my lack of homemaking skills or my inability to complete a project to my "ADHD." This was a weakness, but I was feeding the weakness by allowing it to determine my behavior. Instead of trying to manage it, I was allowing it to manage me!

I finally realized that God would never put me in a situation without giving me the strength, wisdom, and resources to overcome it. I had to "own up" to my irresponsibility and allow God's strength to pour through this weakness. I dug into the Word of God and was convinced that I needed to be more responsible and manage my life and my environment with more wisdom. Instead of leaving the sink full of dirty dishes, I had to force myself to wash them all before moving on to the next thing that got my attention. Instead of dumping the clean laundry on the bed and leaving the room, I had to force myself to fold it before walking away. It was difficult to develop those "habits of completion," but it got easier and easier every day. Now, it just comes naturally; and He has blessed my efforts and my obedience above and beyond what I ever expected.

It's easy to blame a weakness, and you will always be able to find an excuse for every fault. But, if you rely on God's power in your weakness and lift your behavior to a higher standard, then you'll be shocked at the wonderful works God can do through you. It is only through His power that I can manage to do all the tasks I do during the day. In my own power, I never could. This is a super-power that comes straight from God!

So, What's the Secret?
Everyone always wants to know the "secret" behind superheroes. What is the source of Superman's strength? Why does Thor carry around a hammer? How does Wonder Woman get her hair to stay like that? When you begin to let God develop super powers through your life as a mom, people are going to begin to wonder. I get it all the time—"How do you do it all?" "What's your secret?" When I tell them that it is God working through me, they lose their curiosity a bit. Now, if I told them that the secret is to gobble like a turkey three times every morning and eat twenty-two peanuts, they would probably go try it out. (please don't try this at home). People just want quick fixes. They want the radioactive spider bite! That's the kind of culture we live in—quick, easy, and no effort on our part.

God may be popular today, but I've found that a lot of people just want to take bits and pieces of Him, roll them up in a ball, and call it "God." As long as God is convenient, they will worship Him. Well, there is nothing convenient about God. He is not there to serve us. We are here to glorify Him. When we really understand this principle, it frees us up to live a super-powered life. This is the secret. It's all about Him. It's not anything we can do; but everything that He does through us.

Understand this one principle and life will go so much easier for you—you have weak spots and that is exactly how God created you. He created you with these weaknesses so you would need Him. And when you let His power pour through those weak spots and when you let His healing mend your brokenness, you are actually stronger and more powerful than you ever could become on your own. It's so amazing! And it's something that only God can do. He doesn't do this because He is on a power trip. He does this because He wants *you* to be on a power trip. He loves you and He wants an abundant, joyful, glorious life for you. But it is not something you can do on your own. You can only accomplish this kind of life through the power of God.

The absolutely coolest thing about all this is that when God is in control and pouring His power through us, we get more done in less time with less resources. It works this way because He's in charge and He's calling the shots, not you.

One time, my brother-in-law, Sheldon, was trying to make some homemade wine. Evidently, he had come across a book on making wine and decided to embark on a new career. He collected all the necessary ingredients and carefully followed the directions in the book. Well, almost. He left out the part regarding the need for proper sealing equipment because he didn't want to spend the money and thought it was pretty useless. Then, he placed the concoction in his dark closet to allow it to ferment. After the necessary two weeks, he invited all of his friends over for the big unveiling. He went into his closet and pulled out the bottles. With all of his friends gathered around him, he pried open the cork and—lo and behold—the putrid-smelling concoction was full of maggots! There was certainly no wine tasting that evening, I promise you that! Sheldon spent money, time, and energy and ended up with a disgusting mess that he had to throw away. Then on top of that, he was stuck making a run to the liquor store!

This kind of stuff doesn't happen when God is in charge. Jesus was a guest at a wedding once. When they ran out of wine, Mary, Jesus' mom, called him over and told everyone around, "Whatever he tells you to do, do it." Jesus then told them to fill up the jars with water. They obeyed and in only a moment, Jesus turned that water into wine. But not just any old wine, the finest wine you ever tasted! Just goes to show you what can happen when you obey your mama!

That's what happens when God is in charge. We can spin our wheels all day trying to accomplish something—whether it's raising our kids to be more obedient, managing our money better, improving our marriage, or whatever—and end up going no where! If God isn't directing our efforts, it's a waste of our time, money, and energy. Think about how long it takes to make wine…first you've got to get the grapes, then turn them into juice, then age the stuff (with the right equipment, please). And the better the wine, the longer it takes. Then Jesus steps onto the scene and in moments, He produces the finest wine ever tasted—out of nothing but water! When God is in charge, it can happen *in a moment*. And it doesn't just turn out right. It turns out better than you could imagine! He only asks one thing—obedience. Jesus used plain old water, but the people had to fill up the jars on their own. He can use whatever you've got. You don't have to scramble around trying to find the right resources or the best connections. You've already got whatever He needs to use. He just needs your obedience. Whatever He asks you to do, do it. A miracle is waiting.

Grown, Not Given
No doubt about it, it's hard to grow kids. Every single age brings its own set of challenges. Toddlers are especially infamous about keeping us on our toes. I remember when our firstborn, Kelsey, was learning how to walk. I was maniacal about her safety! We didn't have enough money to buy those plastic corner protectors so I hot glued Styrofoam and folded up pieces of bubble wrap to all the furniture in the house! It's not like it messed up the furniture, because all we had were old castoff pieces that I found in thrift stores or dumpster diving. However, the Styrofoam and bubble wrap sure didn't help the aesthetics of our tiny little apartment. I couldn't teach her how to walk without hurting herself, but I was sure going to do all I could to keep her safe.

It would be nice if our babies could just stand up one day and start walking, but it doesn't work that way. It's a process. They have to grow into their walking feet. But thank goodness they are hardheaded and never stop trying until they get it right.

It would be a shame if your baby tried to walk one day, fell on his bee-hind, and then decided to never give it another go. Think of everything he would miss out on—running, dancing, playing superheroes with his brothers. There's no doubt about it, the effort is worth it (even the spills, bumps, and occasional collisions with bubble wrap). But so many of us do that! We set out to improve our lives and make positive changes, and then give it up just when it gets challenging enough to build our skills.

God does not give us super powers. He grows them in us. I used to be very short-tempered with my kids. I would pray that God would make me more patient and understanding in the morning, and by the afternoon, I had kids throwing fits left and right. I had to grow into patience and it would have never happened if I had perfectly behaved kids every minute of the day. It happens when times get rough and I have to depend on God to pour His power through me. In every challenging situation, when we choose to be victors instead of victims, we become stronger. That's how we develop our super powers.

"Blessed (happy, fortunate, prosperous, and enviable) is the man who walks and lives not in the counsel of the ungodly [following their advice, their plans and purposes], nor stands [submissive and inactive] in the path where sinners walk, nor sits down [to relax and rest] where the scornful [and the mockers] gather. But his delight and desire are in the law of the Lord, and on His law (the precepts, the instructions, the teachings of God) he habitually meditates (ponders and studies) by day and by night. And he shall be like a tree firmly planted [and tended] by the streams of water, ready to bring forth its fruit in its season; its leaf also shall not fade or wither; and everything he does shall prosper [and come to maturity]." Psalm 1:1-3

Think about it. Do you know people who seem "happy, fortunate, prosperous, enviable"? It's not just luck and it doesn't just *happen*. It's those super powers that have been grown through the discipline and diligence to live within the boundaries that God has set for our lives. And if you want what they've got, you've got to be willing to do what they've done to get it.

God is not some kind of "spoil sport," wanting to drain all the fun out of life. As a matter of fact, it's quite the opposite! God sets boundaries for us and provides us with challenges so that we can develop all those qualities that this passage describes—blessed, happy, fortunate, prosperous, and enviable. God's people should be the happiest people on earth! Our lives aren't ones of denial. They are some serious, knock-down, drag-out FUN!

This scripture tells us that when we choose to follow God's ways instead of the advice, plans, and purposes that go against what He wants for us, and when we habitually meditate on God's word, then we will be like a tree firmly planted by the water. We will yield fruit in season, never fading or withering, and *everything we do will prosper*. God never makes a promise that He won't fulfill and this is definitely a promise worth taking Him up on! But, like this passage states, we will yield this fruit in season. These qualities are not just given to us; they are grown in us.

God grows those super powers in us, but we have a responsibility, too. We have to follow God's commands for our lives, to give up those habits or desires that we know do not glorify Him. We have to develop habits of digging deep in His Word and not just casually glancing in our Bibles on Sundays when the preacher tells us to look up something. *Habitually* means we do it when we feel like and when we don't. It takes diligence and discipline. Then in season (that means after our time of sowing and after we weather a few rainstorms), we will find those super powers being grown in us in remarkable ways. *Everything we do will prosper*—that means raising our kids, growing our marriage, managing our money, living a healthy life, taking care of our homes, even developing those talents and skills that we didn't even realize were planted inside of us!

So, What is Your Superhero Costume?

Wouldn't it be cool to go around in a superhero costume every day? We could dust the furniture in a sexy little get-up with shiny boots, spandex tights, and a flowing cape to top it all off! (I'm pretty sure my kids would have a serious problem with that.) But, have you ever wondered why superheroes have to wear costumes that are tight, stretchy, and super cool? Maybe with fins on their gloves or a big letter on their chest? I mean, sure, it looks awesome and all…but why can't a superhero do superhero-y things wearing jeans, a t-shirt, and a worn-out pair of Keds?

Basically, they wear those outfits so that you can tell them apart from the regular people. It identifies them as being a superhero and not just some Joe Schmoe off the street. Think about it, if Superman wore a suit and tie, he would just be this newspaper photographer flying around all over the place and lifting trains off their tracks. That would just be a little too weird! Instead, he has to transform! He rips that shirt off and exposes that big red "S" on his chest. Before you know it, he's flying around in his blue tights saving people left and right.

We're no different. There is a superhero inside each one of us, but we've got to transform *first*. One of my favorite verses in the Bible is Romans 12:2. God has spoken to me through this verse in so many ways:

> *"Do not be conformed to this world (this age), [fashioned after and adapted to its external, superficial customs], but be transformed (changed) by the [entire] renewal of your mind [by its new ideals and its new attitude], so that you may prove [for yourselves] what is the good and acceptable and perfect will of God, even the thing which is good and acceptable and perfect [in His sight for you]." Romans 12:2*

If you are ever going to see super powers grow in your life, you must first be transformed. You've got to rip off the clothes of this world (not literally, so don't go stripping down to your undies). We are so trained to think in terms of our current culture—how to raise our kids, handle our marriage, perform at our job, manage our homes, even spend our money! We need to quit thinking and acting like the world and start conforming to the image of Christ. This means getting new ideals and fresh attitudes that are in agreement with God. Then, and only then, will we ever see God's supernatural power at work in our lives.

As a Christian, people are looking at you, wondering what's different. Superheroes are recognized by their cool costumes. We must be recognized by our new way of life. If people are talking bad about someone, don't join in. Be the one to start a new conversation. If the salesman is trying to convince you to spend money you don't have, be strong enough to obey your principals and refuse to go into debt. Every day there are opportunities to show off your superhero suit. Don't conform—be transformed!

When I first started out doing media—writing books, doing television appearances, and being a spokesperson for companies, I busted my bee-hind trying to get publicity. I drove myself crazy sending out tons of emails every day, coming up with story ideas and sending them to network shows, and spending hours online searching for angles left and right. I tried everything to get my name out there and get some face time in newspapers and on television. I even hired a publicist (that I couldn't afford). This went on for month after agonizing month, wracking my brain trying to get publicity and going nowhere. And when I say "nowhere," I mean it. My uber-expensive publicist was able to drum up a few stories on a local radio station here and there, but that's about it. My story ideas kept going out and getting zero response. I couldn't understand it. I was doing everything that every business manual and "how to get publicity" article told me to do; and what did I get for it? A big, fat nothin'!

Finally, God spoke to me and told me to lay off. I was conforming to the pattern of this world. I was doing the customary rituals instead of putting all my trust in God. The next day, I fired my publicist (and had to spend the next six month paying her off in installments—talk about punishment for my sins!!). I also quit paying for press kits I couldn't afford. Instead of spending hours on the computer trying to get publicity, I spent hours with my children—dong school projects, cooking up stuff in the kitchen, and playing around. The stress was gone. Even though I didn't know how I was going to get publicity, I had the peace of mind that if anything was going to happen with my business, it was going to be God doing it and not me. I had to transform my heart before God could ever transform my business.

The funniest part of all this was after a few months of "hands off" I was contacted by the *Today* show and asked if I could come on the show! After I finally caught my breath, I told them in no uncertain terms, "YES!" I couldn't even drum up attention from a local radio station; and here comes God bringing the *Today* show to my doorstep. It's so true, we can only know the best of what God wants for us and really experience those super powers at work when we stop conforming to this world and become renewed by God in our hearts and minds.

Where is my Super Suit?
I love the movie, *The Incredibles*. It's about a family of superheroes who have to go into hiding until the day that "Syndrome" decides to force his evil will on the world. One of my favorite parts is when one of their family friends, also a superhero, sees chaos breaking out in the town square outside his apartment window. Suddenly, he's running around the place, hollering at his wife, "Honey! Where is my super suit?" She's hollering back that he doesn't need it anymore because he's retired. "I must protect the greater good!" he hollers back. Then you hear her voice from down the hall, "Greater good? *I am* your greater good!"

We're not ready to do battle until we're dressed in our super suits. This is a conscious thing all of us must do if we are ever going to see our super powers grow. In this entire process of growing our super powers, we are partners with God. We have the responsibility of becoming more like His Son, Jesus, and studying His Word. And He takes care of everything else! We become more like Jesus as we strip off the behaviors and attitudes of this world and develop the character qualities that set us apart as believers. Paul described this process like this:

"...you have stripped off the old (unregenerate) self with its evil practices, and have clothed yourselves with the new [spiritual self], which is [ever in the process of being] renewed and remolded into [fuller and more perfect [knowledge upon] knowledge after the image (the likeness) of Him Who created it." Colossians 3:9-10

The definition of regenerate is to be made over, reconstituted or re-created in a better form. This is what happens when God gets a hold of your life. You are re-created from the inside out in a better form. And one of the coolest things about this process is that it never, ever stops. Thank goodness! Because, at least for me, it seems like I never stop messing up. None of us will ever be perfect. We'll never be just like Christ. Instead, we are continually being "perfected" as we strive to be more like Him.

This isn't just some magical transformation, like the fairy godmother did when she turned Cinderella's raggedy old dress into a beautiful ball gown. It's a conscious thing that we have to do every single day (sometimes, every single minute!). We have to make a choice to "put on" the characteristics of Jesus. Just like we put on a pair of jeans or a blouse, we have to make a decision to put on kindness, faithfulness, goodness, love, joy, peace, and all those qualities that are so apparent in Jesus.

"Clothe yourselves therefore, as God's own chosen ones (His own picked representatives), [who are] purified and holy and well-beloved [by God Himself, by putting on behavior marked by] tenderhearted pity and mercy, kind feeling, a lowly opinion of yourselves, gentle ways, [and] patience [which is tireless and long-suffering, and has the power to endure whatever comes, with good temper]. Be gentle and forbearing with one another and, if one has a difference (a grievance or complaint) against another, readily pardoning each other; even

as the Lord has [freely] forgiven you, so must you also [forgive]. And above all these [put on] love and enfold yourselves with the bond of perfectness [which binds everything together completely in ideal harmony]." Colossians 3:12-14

    This is a pretty tall order. But God would never put a task before you that He won't also empower you to perform. You were hand-picked by God! He has chosen you to live an amazing life and He is more than enough to make that happen. But, it's a two-way street. You have to get dressed, Mama! This passage above describes qualities that we have to get dressed in—like kindness, humility, gentleness, patience, forgiveness, and love. These qualities are called "fruit" in the Bible because they are grown in our lives, through a supernatural combination of God's power and our habits. You make a habit of consciously putting them on; and through God's power it becomes easier and easier over time. We're taking it step-by-step in this book; and my prayer for you is that pretty soon you will be shocked at how competent God has made you to live a life with passion, purpose, and power.

The Superhero Manual
How do superheroes even know how to be superheroes? Are they just born awesome? We have a pretty big collection of family movies here in the house. One movie that my kids have watched over and over is "Sky High." It's about a high school for superheroes. They have to take classes and perform feats so they can eventually graduate and become actual heroes. The entire cheerleading squad was just one superhero girl who had the power to duplicate herself.
    We can't just expect to develop our super powers without doing some study on the side. God's Word contains every bit of information we will ever need to prosper on all levels in our lives. It tells us how to raise our kids, manage our money, strengthen our marriages, and everything else that we need to know. You like "how to" manuals? Well, this is the ultimate one!

But, it's not just a book. It's the living, breathing Word of God. Check out what the Bible can do:

"The Word of God, which is effectually at work in you who believe [exercising its superhuman power in those who adhere to and trust in and rely on it]." I Thessalonians 2:13

When you adhere to, trust in, and rely on the Word of God something miraculous happens—SUPERHUMAN powers! Now, *that's* what I'm talking about! As you dig deep in His Word and really spend time studying, you get results.

For a few years, I thought I was too busy as a mom to study God's Word. I would glance in a devotion book once a day or spend a few minutes in prayer; but as far as spending real time and energy into studying the Bible? No way! I just didn't have the time. After a long while, I finally realized that I wasn't seeing results in my life. I kept wanting God's direction in my life and desiring to do His will, but nothing was happening. Well, nothing positive, that is. I was getting more and more overwhelmed with my schedule. I was sinking into debt. I was losing my patience with my kids. It wasn't pretty. I was busy, all right—busy messing up my life!

Finally, I realized that I was pleading with God for results and wanting Him to work in my life; but I was refusing to pick up the manual and learn from it. I began to get up at 6am to I could spend an hour studying the Bible. Believe me, if you have a picture of something like Snow White arising from bed with a smile and a song and a bluebird perched on her shoulder, think again! It was miserable for me when I first began. I was tired and grumpy. I needed a cup of coffee before I could even focus on a page. Sometimes, I would even begin to nod off as I read scripture. There were actually a couple of times that I fell asleep on my Bible, kind of like a high school kid in study hall! It was hard for me because it was change. And you'll find that whenever you make a positive change in your life, your flesh will battle you every step of the way. The best habits to have are the ones that are the most difficult to create.

Then something incredible happened. Not at first, but after I persisted day after day after day. I began to see results, fast! God was really speaking to me and giving me direction through His Word. I would want to snap at my husband, and then recall a verse that I had studied about how the power of life and death is in the tongue. I would want to buy something that was out of my budget and would recall a verse about how I should lend and not borrow. Pretty soon, I was seeing such amazing results in my attitudes, thoughts, and insights, that I started getting up at 5:30 so I could spend another half hour in Bible study.

You want to know the absolute coolest thing about it all? I found that as I spent more time studying the Bible, I actually got more done with the rest of my day. It was like that verse talked about—His Word was <u>effectually</u> at work in me (I Thess. 2:13). It wasn't just something to read and study. It was something that was changing my life and creating tangible results. I was hooked.

Give me Five!
You're like Korben's superhero character, Five. There's nothing he can't do! And there is nothing that God cannot do through you. God has a wonderful plan for your life and He has everything lined up to make it happen! He has super powers stored up for you, and He's ready to pour them *into* your life and *through* your life. You may have thought that superheroes were just in movies and comic books. No such thing! Look in a mirror. You were created to be a superhero. It is in your DNA. God placed it in you and is more than able to perfect it through you.

I declare that incredible ability is rising up in you right now. Seeds are being planted in you that will yield an abundant harvest in every area of your life. You will have the strength to make the right choices with your words, your actions, and your resources. You will create habits of excellence in your life. No matter what challenge lies before you or within you, God will pour His supernatural power and ability through you and you will be blessed—not just a little blessing, but an over-the-top Hulk size blessing!

CRAZY BONUS!
You may not know this, but stress is NOT a super power.
If you struggle with stress, make sure you do my 21-Day Mom
Rescue. It will knock that stress right out of you!
Use the coupon code, RESCUE20 and get over
HALF off the regular price! Wooohooo!
Just go to www.21daymomrescue.com

STEP 8

GIVE WHAT YOU WANT TO GET

There are definite advantages to living on several acres of woods. First of all, my kids can be as loud as they want without neighbors calling the authorities. With seven noisy kids, that's definitely a plus. Also, we can dispose of biodegradable stuff right here in our backyard. After Christmas, all my husband has to do with the tree is take down all the ornaments and drag it to the woods. Pretty easy, right? Another advantage is my kids get to roam in the woods to their hearts' content. On any pretty day, you will find them stomping in the creek, throwing rocks in the pond, or balancing on the trunk of a fallen tree. It's a great thing to live in the woods (well, aside from the raccoons that have a personal vendetta against our trashcans!).

    The kids are always bringing back odd finds from their jaunts in the woods. One day it could be a beautiful, silver-flecked rock; another day, it could be an abandoned whiskey bottle. One day, Klara and Kenna stumbled across a very rare find—a Christmas tree (I didn't have the heart to tell them that their daddy had dragged it out there about eight months earlier)! They were so excited about their tree, and promptly "planted" it in the front yard, right in the middle of my petunia bed!

    As if that wasn't enough, they decided to make it a "holiday" tree and collected as many decorations as they could find in the basement, pulled them out, and donned the tree with them. They even dragged out the craft supplies and made more. There were red construction paper hearts, a strand of green clover lights, a red, white, and blue paper chain, and a big scarecrow sitting on the ground in front. Not exactly what you would find on HGTV, but it was definitely festive!

After a couple days, I was getting ready to broach the topic of extracting the tree. That's when Klara and Kenna came inside after playing and asked, "Mama, why isn't our tree growing?"

I looked out the window at that dead, multi-colored monstrosity, and said, "Well, girls, that tree is dead. It was chopped down, so it's not going to grow anymore."

I saw their faces fall and immediately said, "But I love the way you decorated it. It's so pretty! And it's right there on our front lawn for all our guests to see!"

They beamed in pride.

I was forced to leave it up another two weeks.

Pipes Not Buckets
It's a law that has been in effect since the beginning of time—you reap what you sow. If you plant sunflower seeds, you get sunflowers. If you plant watermelon seeds you get watermelon. And if you plant a dead Christmas tree, you're going to end up with a dead Christmas tree. You can dress it up all you want, but it's still a dead Christmas tree. Sowing and reaping is a universal concept, and you can see it all throughout scripture:

"[Remember] this: he who sows sparingly and grudgingly will also reap sparingly and grudgingly, and he who sows generously [that blessing may come to someone] will also reap generously and with blessings." 2 Corinthians 9:6

It's such a simple concept, really. Here's the deal: You get what you give. It's that easy. Do everything in your power to make sure you are a blessing to others, and you will get blessed in return. But, our human nature gets it all inside-out and backwards. We have the tendency to want to "look out for number one" and believe that you get ahead by pushing yourself ahead. That's not the case at all. Check out that verse. When you sow generously so that blessing may come to someone, you will also reap generously and with blessings! Do you want to be blessed? Then be a blessing!

This is where a lot of people nod in agreement, and then go out to the parking lot and get mad if they don't get spot near the entrance, or get frustrated if they don't get good service at the restaurant. Don't let this concept pass you by, as it does for most people. If you have read this far, you are NOT most people. You want to be blessed and you're willing to do what needs to be done to make that happen. Well, this is what needs to be done. You need to *be* a blessing.

My kids are notorious for mixing up some concoctions outside, and using my good pots and pans for the job! After a while, I'll notice that one of my pots has gone missing, and I have to hunt around outside to find it. Inevitably, it's full of a mucky, nasty sludge. I have to give it a mighty good cleaning before it's ever fit to use again! That's what happens when stuff *collects*. It gets stale and nasty. You were not placed here on earth to collect. You are here to be a channel. When you let blessing flow into your life, and never let it flow out to others, it will eventually stop flowing. And any blessing that is collected in your life will stagnate and turn putrid. God is movement. God is expansion. And God cannot be contained.

God is looking for pipes where His blessing can flow through, not buckets that will just collect and grow stale. When you are a blessing, God will move mountains to make sure that blessing keeps on flowing into your life. That's the reason why when you sow generously, you also reap generously. God sees to it. Your job is to be a blessing. God's job is to bless. You do your job and He'll do His.

Pure Gold

You can use this simple formula to get what you want in life. It works like a charm, every single time. The Golden Rule is "Do unto others as you would have them do unto you" (Luke 6:31). And the inverse of this is also a rule: "Others will do unto you as you do unto them." The thing with God's rules is that they cannot be broken! So, why not use this to your advantage and put this rule to work for you?

For example, if you want more respect from your husband, then you can do things the human way and gripe about how he doesn't help you around the house and nag at him until he reluctantly picks up his underwear off the floor of the bathroom. Or you could do things God's way and sow what you want to reap. If you want respect, then start pouring it on thick! Honor him in everything he does. Encourage him every chance you get. And, yes, pick his underwear up off the floor!

Some of you are thinking, "No way! That would just give him permission to do it all the time and think that it's okay to have me picking up after him." Honey, that's exactly what Satan wants you to believe. But, listen to the wisdom of God:

"There are those who [generously] scatter abroad, and yet increase more; there are those who withhold more than is fitting or what is justly due, but it results only in want. The liberal person shall be enriched, and he who waters shall himself be watered." Proverbs 11: 24,25

That's God talking, so listen up. It doesn't make sense in our human wisdom (or lack thereof), but that's how God works. When you give generously, you will increase. But if you withhold blessing from others, it will result in want! The main reason so many people find themselves wanting and wishing, is because they are withholding the very thing they are striving so hard to get their hands on. It doesn't seem logical, does it? It seems like if you want more money, you should be stingy and hold on to every penny that comes your way. If you want more time, you should never volunteer to help others. But that's not how it works at all.

I remember when Blair and I didn't think we had enough money to tithe. Well, you and I both know by now that was just an excuse. And there is one thing I've learned about excuses: *An excuse is a lie we create to protect us from a truth we are unwilling to accept.* The excuse? We didn't have enough money to give away 10%. The truth? We were unwilling to change our lifestyle to free up enough money to tithe. It wasn't like we were living "high on the hog," as we say here in the south. In actuality,

131

we were barely scraping by. We had debts to pay off and rationalized that we could pay them off faster if we didn't give away ten percent.

Living by this wisdom (or lack of it) only resulted in us continuing to scrape by and dig our financial hole deeper and deeper each month. Finally, we stopped trying to do things *our* way, and decided to try *God's* way for a change. We took the plunge and began tithing, ten percent right off the top. It didn't make a bit of sense to us at the time, but we were trusting that God's Word was truth and we were going to follow directions. If it's true that the man who sows generously will also reap generously, then God's way was the only way we were going to get out of our money mess.

It didn't happen right away. But, somehow, each month, we had just enough money to make ends meet. We didn't get to splurge, but we weren't going further into debt. And the best part was that the stress and worry was gone. Now it was no longer our problem. It was God's. When we dedicated ourselves to giving and managing our money God's way, we rolled all that care and concern over on to Him. What a relief!

We began to notice that things were just taken care of. Cars stayed working. Appliances didn't break down. Clothes didn't need to be replaced. As soon as a need would surface, the supply was right there, as if it had been placed there by God Himself (and it had!). One year, my daughter wanted some black high-top tennis shoes for her birthday. We didn't have the money to buy them, so I began looking around for various solutions, but I couldn't come up with anything! Then one day, I got a text from my sister. It was a picture of a pair of beautiful black high-top tennis shoes, a better brand than I would ever consider buying, with the question, "Would Klara like these shoes?" Evidently, her daughter had outgrown them before she could ever get some good use out of them.

My heart leaped for joy! I started crying, right there, looking at that picture on my phone. It was as if God was telling me, "Trust me! I've got everything taken care of." I wasn't crying because she got to get the shoes she wanted. I was crying because of God's thoughtfulness to the tiniest details. He longs to show Himself mighty on your behalf. He longs to pour blessings in to your life. He's just looking for the pipes He can use. Are you going to be one of those pipes?

Don't ever fall for Satan's trap to get you to cling to your possessions, money, time, and skill. Don't ever withhold kindness, love, gratitude, and service. If you have an opportunity to give, then do it! Satan wants nothing good for you, so don't listen to his lies that if you give it away you won't ever get it back. That's his tactic to get you to live in lack. Satan knows what would happen in your life if you started being a blessing to everyone who comes within your reach, and he doesn't want any of that! Listen to God instead. Give generously and watch it come back to you in waves!

You need to remember something important about this principle—when you are giving to others, you are giving to God. When you are serving others, you are actually serving God. And when you give, He gives back more. God knows where the gold is, and He's more than willing to pour it into your life. You cannot out-give God! Think about that next time you don't want to pick up your husband's underwear or have to clean up that mess your child made in the kitchen! You're doing it for God, and He is the One Who rewards you—big time!

The Rules of the Harvest
When it comes to sowing and reaping, every gardener knows there are certain rules that apply. You abide by these rules and you'll reap a harvest every single time. And here they are:

* Rule One: Plant in Good Soil

I remember moving to the deserts of Arizona after living in South Carolina my entire life. One of the first things I did was go out and pick up a bunch of azaleas and plant them all around my house. Well, it wasn't any time at all before that scorching desert sun and those soaring temperatures killed off those azaleas. They were great plants, but I had planted them in desert sand. They didn't stand a chance! Jesus talked about the importance of sowing into good soil—

"Give attention to this! Behold, a sower went out to sow. And as he was sowing, some seed fell along the path, and the birds came and ate it up.

Other seed [of the same kind] fell on ground full of rocks, where it had not much soil; and at once it sprang up, because it had no depth of soil; and when the sun came up, it was scorched, and because it had not taken root, it withered away.

Other seed [of the same kind] fell among thorn plants, and the thistles grew and pressed together and utterly choked and suffocated it, and it yielded no grain.

And other seed [of the same kind] fell into good (well-adapted) soil and brought forth grain, growing up and increasing, and yielded up to thirty times as much, and sixty times as much, and even a hundred times as much as had been sown." Mark 4:3-8

Jesus goes on to explain this parable to his disciples, but basically He's talking about the condition of your heart. There are some that hear the Word and then Satan snatches it away before their thoughts can dwell on it (and he loves to use distraction to do just that). There are some that get an instant thrill about the promises in God's Word, but as soon as any type of trial comes up or they have to wait longer than they thought, they fall away and lose their fire. There are also some that hear the Word and get excited about following God; but the flesh starts waging war. Desires for riches, fame, notoriety, and other earthly pleasures rise up and choke out the Word of God. The ego wins out.

But then there are some who have good soil. They want God more than they want anything else. They want to see His promise fulfilled in their lives and are willing to do what it takes, as long as it takes, until they see that harvest in their lives. This is commitment. And commitment always yields a harvest. How much of a harvest do you want? That totally depends on how committed you're willing to be.

It says in the sower parable, that some get thirty times as much, some sixty times as much, and some even a hundred times as much as had been sown. How much of a harvest do you want? Jesus had thousands that followed Him. Then He had seventy that stuck really close. Twelve were committed enough to be His disciples. Only three were allowed near Him—Peter, James, and John—during times when He needed people who had strong, unwavering faith. But there was one—John—who stuck by His side, even when it meant going to the cross. And because of his level of commitment, John carried so much power that they eventually had to exile him because every attempt to kill him ended in failure. Commitment is rewarding.

Are you going to be one that is kind of committed or *fully committed?* Do you want to get 30, 60 or *one hundred times* the amount you invest? Your harvest depends on you. Keep sowing seeds of kindness, love, mercy, forgiveness, joy, faith, and don't ever stop. Don't give it a time limit and don't put parameters on your giving. Just keep your heart resting in full faith, trusting God for the harvest that you can't see yet.

* Rule Two: Dig It and Forget It

I'm pretty sure we're all guilty of breaking this rule on occasion. It's that tendency to sow your seed and then try to dig it up and see what's happening. One time, as a homeschooling project, the kids planted bean seeds in a clear glass jar with a wet paper towel. It was so cool to see the seed swell, break open, the roots and shoots come out, and watch as they divided and multiplied. But that's not always the case with gardening. Soil is dark for a reason. It's a mystery.

"And He said, The kingdom of God is like a man who scatters seed upon the ground, and then continues sleeping and rising night and day while the seed sprouts and grows and increases—he knows not how. The earth produces [acting] by itself—first the blade, then the ear, then the full grain in the ear." Mark 4:26-27

There are four words in that scripture that have totally changed the way I live. It's the phrase, "he knows not how." When we start sowing good seed in order to reap a harvest, it is always tempting to want to box up God and figure out how He's going to come through with the victory. We may want to change a person, so we begin sowing seed of praying habitually for them. Time goes by, and that person just seems to be getting worse. We may need a financial breakthrough, so we begin sowing seed of tithe to our church and other forms of financial giving. After awhile, there's a stack of bills on our desk that we can't pay and our income isn't growing at all. I'm not sure if there's anything more frustrating than sowing seed and staring at the soil…and staring…and staring…and never seeing any shoot pop out of the ground.

    But you can't see what's going on underneath the soil. That's God's domain, and there's a reason He keeps it a mystery. It's called faith. We dig the hole, plant the seed, cover it up, and forget about it. God's ways are higher than our ways, always have been, always will be. We don't have to know HOW He's going to do something. We just have to have total and complete faith that He will. In His own way, and in His own time, He will. I can assure you, though, that what He comes up with is always way better than anything we could have every imagined.

    A lot of times, when people need a breakthrough in their lives, they will drum up a list of different ways that God can come through for them. Then, they'll hold their little human list up to heaven and say, "Okay, God, pick a miracle, any miracle…" We so desperately want to put our own human wisdom on an infinite, omniscient, all-powerful God, and it just doesn't work. I can tell you from experience that God always comes through, almost never in the way we think He's going to, and always better than we expect. He'll use people we never expect, open doors we never knew existed, and build skills in us we never knew we could possess.

    Our responsibility is to keep caring for the seed that we planted. Stay committed and keep poking around in that dark soil where God is working. You can't see what's going on. Your seed is swelling up and bursting forth. It's got to establish roots before it ever sends out shoots, or else your breakthrough will not have a firm foundation. You just keep watering it with commitment.

Keep weeding it with righteousness. Don't let sin creep in and cause you to doubt. Your God is love; and His Word is truth. You can't doubt a combination like that! And, don't look around and get jealous of someone else's harvest. That's like pouring salt on the soil. Nothing good can come out of sin. Love others. Pray for others. Bless others. And keep sowing your seed.

Check out that last scripture. Your job is to *sow* and *sleep*! That's right. Stick that seed in the ground and then go rest and let God do His thing. His laws will go into effect. You don't need to know HOW. You just need to know WHO. God is in charge of the increase, not you.

* Rule Three: Give It Time

I remember when my parents planted a bunch of ivy all over their front yard. I came to visit them that summer and felt so sorry for them. All they had in their front yard were a bunch of tiny, little shoots of ivy sticking out of the ground. It looked pathetic! The second summer I came to visit, it was growing a tiny bit, but their front yard still looked sparse—like a huge expanse of South Carolina soil with tiny dots of ivy here and there. I asked them if they wanted me to help them do something with their yard while I was visiting, but they waved off my offer.

"Don't worry about it," they said. "It'll grow!" My poor, sweet parents…I felt so sorry for them with that ridiculous looking front yard.

Then the next summer when I came to visit, there was ivy covering their entire front yard. I could hardly recognize it! The entire thing was just a mass of ivy leaves! If you're an avid gardener, then you know there's a saying when it comes to planting ivy. It goes like this—the first year it sleeps, the second year it creeps, and the third year it leaps. My parents certainly proved that saying is true.

All harvests take time. And some of the most bountiful harvests take the longest to grow. Genesis 8:22 tells us that as long as the earth endures, there will be seedtime and harvest. It's more like seed…….time……and harvest. Growth takes time. You can't expect to plant some magic seed, go take a short nap, and then go out and you have a beanstalk shooting straight up to heaven. That only happens in fairy tales. But, God's Word is better than any fairy tale. It always has a better ending and it's all truth!

He is Lord of the harvest. He will bring it to pass. Remember, it takes time to grow strong roots. Proverbs 12:12 tells us that "the root of the [uncompromisingly] righteous yields [richer fruitage]." Do not compromise your faith. Keep believing that God is Who He says He is and will do what He says He will do. I'm just going to let you in on something right now. It's going to probably take longer than you expect. If God poured all that harvest into your life right now, you wouldn't be able to handle it. It needs roots. Give it time and don't set a limit. Just decide right now that you're planting that seed, and you're going to *keep* planting that seed, and you're not going to stop believing for the harvest.

But I'll tell you something that will work like Miracle Gro for your seed—gratitude! Get that seed in the ground. Keep living righteously and stepping forward in faith. Then pour on the gratitude. Instead of staring down at your seed and saying, "Oh, please grow. Please grow!" Stare up at your God and shout, "Thank you, Almighty God, that You are growing my seed!" God already told you it would grow. Trust Him, praise Him, and thank Him that He always comes through! Thankfulness will cause those shoots to leap!

* Rule Four: Pick When It's Ripe

When Katie was a little girl, she decided to take up gardening. Her first experiment was radishes. She put those tiny seeds into the ground and would go out every single day to water her seeds and check on their growth. Pretty soon, she saw tiny little shoots coming out of the ground. Before long, she saw whites of the growing radishes peeking out from the bottom of the soil. When she watered one day, the water pushed the soil away from one of the plants, and she saw a hint of red. That girl got so excited that she pulled that radish out of the ground,

washed it off, and bit off a chunk. Well, she immediate
out because it was so bitter!

You can't harvest the fruit before it's time. It won't be ripe
for anything. It will be bitter and hard. When you begin to see
growth in the seed that you plant, don't rush in and try to harvest
it or you could ruin everything you have been working on. I
knew one woman who had been praying a long time for her
husband to come to faith in Christ. One day, lo and behold, he
got up on Sunday morning and got dressed to go with her to
church. She got so excited that she encouraged him to read his
Bible that night and tried to sign him up for a men's Bible study
class. Well, he refused to get out of bed that next Sunday. She
scared the poor guy off! She pulled that radish out of the ground
and took a big ole bite!

When we start seeing a harvest, sometimes we get so
excited that we try to rush things. But God is still growing and
ripening. And if you want a sweet harvest, you will let go and let
Him do what He does best.

*"But when the grain is ripe and permits, immediately
he sends forth [the reapers] and puts in the sickle, because the
harvest stands ready". Mark 4:29*

The harvest should not surprise you. The farmer doesn't
look out his window one day and say, "Oh my Lord, that corn
seed is sprouting! Can you believe it? It's actually sprouting!"
He's a farmer. He knows the rules of the harvest. You plant the
seed and it grows. He just keeps caring for it until it is fully
ripened. Be grateful when you see the harvest beginning in your
life, but don't rush ahead and try to pick it before it's ready. Just
keep living righteously. Keep caring for the harvest while it's
growing. And when God permits, it will be ready to reap.

The Power of Selflessness

Of all things to sow, I believe love is the most important. I was
making a business trip one day, and when I got to my gate at the
airport, I noticed that the client had booked me in first class. I got
so excited! I was finally going to enjoy plenty of leg room and

get the primo treatment!—good food, good service, and even those moist towels that I can never really figure out what to do with!

Being a first-class passenger, I got to board before anyone else (actually, I'm not really so sure that's a good thing!). So, by the time everyone else was boarding, I was leaning back, enjoying my lemon water, and relaxing with a book. Almost everyone had boarded, when this heavy woman came by with an obvious limp. She passed me by and God immediately called her out to me. I wasn't sure why, but I began praying over her. It seemed as if everyone had boarded, when one of the flight attendants came up to the front of the plane, where the first class passengers were sitting, and began talking to another flight attendant. They were talking in hushed tones, but they were also right by my seat, so I could hardly help but overhear them.

"I don't know what to do. She's saying she can't sit in the seat because it hurts her leg," said the first attendant.

"Well, she has to sit there. There are no other seats on the flight. It's totally full," the other one replied.

The Spirit of God told me what I needed to do. And, there was absolutely nothing in me that wanted to do it. I wanted to relax right there in first class, with my lemon water and my legroom. But God had other plans for me that day. I leaned over and touched the arm of the first attendant to get her attention.

"Excuse me," I said. Both attendants turned around. "Are you talking about that woman that walked past with a limp?"

"Yes," she replied.

"I'd be happy to exchange seats with her," I said. Both attendants stared at me as if I had gone stark-raving mad. My human nature was kicking and screaming in protest. But I shut that inner brat up and stepped out in obedience. Believe me, it wasn't easy. It was a three-hour trip!

"Are you sure?" the first attendant asked.

"Absolutely!" I said. "It's no problem at all!" My inner brat was yelling, "Yes! It is a problem! I never get any breaks! I deserve first class! Give me my moist towel!!!"

I collected my belongings and headed to the back of the plane to exchange seats. The woman looked practically bewildered as I offered her my seat and directed her toward first class. I saw her limp away before settling down into my seat that now felt as if it were proportioned to fit an American Girl doll. My lemon water didn't taste so good after that. But I made myself as comfortable as I could and dug back into my book.

After we landed (three cramped hours later), I noticed as I was getting off the plane, that the woman was still sitting in the first class seat and both attendants were standing beside her. One of the attendants saw me walking down the aisle of the plane and said, "Here she is," to the woman with the limp.

When I came up to the row where she was sitting, I noticed that she had tears streaming down her face. She grabbed my arm and the look in her eyes was enough to shame any brat that was still pitching a fit inside me.

"I didn't know… there were… people like you…in this world," she said through her sobs. "You have…no idea what you…have done…"

That brat inside was now a shade of crimson and hanging her head in the corner.

"It was my pleasure," I told her. "I'm so glad I could help you out."

"But you don't…understand," she said. "I had lost….all hope in God. I believe…again."

That one little favor, that one selfless act—who could have ever known where it would have led? She didn't need a first class seat. She needed to know that God was real and that He still cared about her. He was just using the pipe that was available.

Don't ever underestimate the power of selflessness. When you give, it will be given to you in the same measure—pressed down, shaken together, and spilling out all over the place. Want to be crazy blessed? Then start blessing like crazy!

Time to Plant
You know the rules of the harvest and you know that God is faithful to make your seed grow. Now is the time to plant. Don't

second-guess your giving. Just give. Give kindness. Give love. Give money. Give time. Give encouragement. Give mercy. Give forgiveness. Just give, and watch God do incredible things in your life. Remember, you can't out give God, and I would love to see you try!

    I declare that with every seed you sow, God is going to grow you like never before. As you stay fully committed, God Almighty is going to produce a harvest in your life that will take your breath away. Right now, in the name of Jesus Christ, seed that you have planted is bursting forth in unprecedented growth. Roots are stretching out. Shoots are stretching up. And rich, abundant, fruit is multiplying to be poured into your life and through your life into others. You will see breakthroughs like never before. And you will experience abundance in every area of your life. Your harvest is coming!

CRAZY BONUS!

Are you ready to start sowing?
Check out this FREE video, "Sow What?"
Click on the link <u>RIGHT HERE</u>, or visit
www.hannahkeeley.com/blog/sowwhat

STEP 9
FOLLOW THE BLUEPRINT

My mama makes the best bread pudding in the whole world. In fact, if you look in her recipe collection, you'll find it written out in her perfect cursive handwriting and titled, "The World's Best Bread Pudding." Every time she brings it to church for a luncheon, it's the first dessert dish that is wiped clean. Everyone clamors for it!

One Sunday afternoon, one of the church ladies, Hattie, came up to Mama and asked for the recipe for her famous bread pudding. Now Mama is no recipe hoarder, so she whipped out her church bulletin and wrote the recipe on the back. She had made it so many times, she had it memorized. Hattie was overjoyed when Mama handed her the bulletin and said, "Give me a call and let me know how it turns out, okay?"

Thursday afternoon, Mama got a call. It was Hattie.
"Hey, Mary!" Hattie said over the phone.
"How are you doing, Hattie?" Mama asked.
"Well, I'm fine," Hattie answered. "But, I've got to tell you, Mary, I'm a bit upset with you. I don't think you wrote this recipe down right. You must have left something out."

Number One, you never insult my mama.
Number Two (and this is even more important than Number One), you never insult my mama's cooking.

"Hattie," Mama said, in a tone that was not quite as chipper as the one she had before. "I wrote down the right recipe. Why don't you tell me how you made it so we can figure out what you did wrong?"

Don't you love the way Mama cleverly turned it around to Hattie's fault? This skill comes with years of working in ministry and raising five children to adulthood. You learn how to avoid taking blame.

"Okay," Hattie began. "Well, I followed the recipe just like you wrote it down."

"You used all the right ingredients?" Mama asked.

"Yes ma'am, I sure did. Well, except…" There was a pause in Hattie's voice. "You know we're on a low cholesterol diet, Mary. So, I just replaced those eggs with Eggbeaters. That's okay, right?"

"I'm not sure, Hattie," Mama answered.

"And I couldn't even figure out what that fancy bread was that you wrote down. I just used the Wonder bread we already had in the pantry," Hattie confessed.

Mama, was beginning to figure out what the problem was.

"And we didn't have any butter," Hattie continued. "So I just used margarine instead. We never use butter because of Frank's high cholesterol."

Hattie kept going, "And you wrote down 'freshly squeezed lemons' but I always use the bottled lemon juice instead. It's practically the same thing. But, Mary, I'm telling you, it didn't taste anything like the one you bring to church. We just ended up throwing it out! The dogs didn't even want to eat it."

"Hattie," Mama said. " I think I know what went wrong."

It's All in the Recipe

Behind every great dish is a great recipe. You follow the recipe; you're going to get the dish. But if you deviate, even a little bit, well…there's no telling what you'll end up with. It could be like that mess that Hattie made and ended up throwing out. If you're going to get anywhere in life, you're going to have to learn how to follow directions.

Pride keeps us in bondage. Pride is what convinces us that we don't need to follow directions, that we can figure out a better way on our own. Pride makes us think we can cut corners and use Wonder bread and still get the same results as someone who takes the time and energy to go to the bakery and pick up a loaf of Challah. But it doesn't work that way. If you want success in life, you're going to have to find the recipe and follow it to the "T."

There is a recipe for success in life. God took the time to write it all out for us in His Word. See, this may go against your personal theology, but God doesn't want us to suffer through life. That was Jesus' job. He took the suffering that should be ours, and in return, He gave us joy, peace, prosperity, and abundance in every area of life. Jesus explained that in this life we will have suffering, but we can choose to live above that suffering because of what He did for us.

"I have told you these things, so that in Me you may have [perfect] peace and confidence. In the world you have tribulation and trials and distress and frustration; but be of good cheer [take courage; be confident, certain, undaunted]! For I have overcome the world. [I have deprived it of power to harm you and have conquered it for you.]" John 16:33

How's that for a reason to rejoice? Sure, trouble will come at us left and right, but it cannot touch us because of the covenant blessing that is on our lives. Jesus already took all the punishment and suffering that should be ours, so we have no excuse to live a life that is anything less than abundant. Satan can threaten, yell, scream, and throw a fit, but he cannot touch you!

I truly think many people just tolerate a below average life because they have learned not to expect anything more. Well, you get what you expect in life, not what you want. So, if you keep on expecting suffering, lack, and misery, you're just going to keep on getting more of the same. I also think people hold on to misery because they're secretly afraid to get their hopes up. What if they get all excited and hope for something better, and it never turns up? Well, I'm asking you, what if you get your hopes up and it does? Isn't that a gamble worth taking?

Success is yours for the taking. Jesus died for you to live—not an "okay" life, but an abundant, over-the-top, crazy blessed life! It's time to get your hopes up and get what's coming to you. Blessing is your birthright, but you've got to follow the recipe if you ever want to get it. So, shut your pride up! It's that part of you that makes you think you should be able to figure this thing out on your own. That's not true. If we knew instinctively how to live a blessed life, everyone in the world would be living in abundance. God knew we needed help ever since we took a bite of that beautiful fruit that belonged to Him. That's why He provided a success recipe. You follow the recipe; you get the results. Every. Single. Time.

God has extreme blessing laid out for you, but only if you follow His blueprint to make it happen. His Word lays out a specific blueprint on how to handle everything in life--relationships, parenting, finances, career, you name it! I want to see you blessed. I consider it my personal responsibility to see that you are equipped to not only tackle every challenge that lies before you, but to reach success in every area of your life. That's why I want to encourage you to do things God's way. Follow His blueprint. He didn't give us commandments to restrict us. He gave them to bless us. When we do things His way, He has promised that He will bless us like crazy!

God never expected us to figure it out on our own. That's why He gave us His Word. That's the blueprint! The truth is, anyone can follow directions. I remember when my son got his first big Lego kit. It was on his eighth birthday and Blair's parents had given it to him. I'm telling you, that kit was huge! I looked at the picture on the front of the box and thought in my mind, 'there is no way that little boy can figure out how to build that huge spaceship.' But, sure enough, he surprised me. He wasn't at all fazed by the challenge. He just dumped out all the pieces and picked up the instruction booklet that came inside the package. Step One, done! Step Two, done! On and on he went until a couple hours had passed, and there was an enormous spaceship parked on our dining room table.

God gives all of us dreams. And He placed within us

everything to make that dream happen. But we have to build it, brick by brick. Thankfully, He also gave us the instruction manual. Korben could have tried to make that spaceship on his own, but he would have probably just spent the entire day frustrated, angry, and disappointed. And he probably would have never been able to do it correctly. Many people are spending their lives just like that—frustrated, angry, and disappointed. That's because they're trying to figure it out on their own. God never meant for that to happen. God's wisdom always trumps man's wisdom. No matter where the challenge is—your marriage, your home, your career, your ministry, your children, your finances—God laid out a step-by-step plan on how to prosper and live in abundance. You can dig into the Word of God and follow His directions, or you can keep on beating your head against the wall. Your choice.

    I've found people want the blessing, but not so much the obedience. For example, you may want a successful marriage, but you may not be so crazy about showing humility and honor to your spouse (especially when it's not returned). You may want to be financially prosperous, but cutting coupons, eating at home every evening, and tithing ten percent doesn't seem to be getting you anywhere. It doesn't always seem to make sense when we do things God's way, but remember, He's in charge of the blessing, not you. You don't have to figure it out. You just have to follow directions.

Which One Are You?
You're probably familiar with the parable of the talents. Jesus told a story of a man who went away and entrusted his money (talents) to his three servants. He gave five talents (probably about five bags of gold) to the first servant, two talents to the second one, and one talent to the third. The first two servants went out and put that money to work and earned even more. But the last servant took the lazy way out. He dug a hole in the ground, tossed that bag in, and left the money to rot. Many of us would think he did that so he could just avoid work and relax. I remember hearing this story when I was younger, and believing

the whole time that it was a warning against taking it easy. In my mind I equated laziness with lying around and not being busy. But that's not true at all. Laziness isn't relaxing under a palm tree in the Caribbean. Laziness is absolute misery! Laziness is that gnawing feeling that you're not living your best life, but you're too scared or confused to do anything about it. So, you drown yourself with distraction to get some temporary relief.

I see people all the time who have been given incredible gifts by God and are not putting them to use and growing their skills and abilities. They aren't hanging around taking it easy. In fact, it's just the opposite. They're usually miserable in their lack of productivity. This last servant probably spent his days worrying about what was going to happen when he had to be accountable, and trying to find excuses for his lack of results.

Well, inevitably, the master returned from his trip and called his servants to him to find out what they did with the money. Take note, friends. There will always be a time of accountability! The first servant pulled out ten bags of gold, doubling his money. Check out the master's response:

"His master said to him, Well done, you upright (honorable, admirable) and faithful servant! You have been faithful and trustworthy over a little; I will put you in charge of much. Enter into and share the joy (the delight, the blessedness) which your master enjoys." Matthew 26:21

How's THAT for a response? First of all, any of us would think three bags of gold was a lot. But in God's economy, it's just a drop in the bucket. This scripture refers to it as "a little." Understand this: God's resources are unlimited. Everything you need to prosper on this earth is already here. He just has to grow your muscles to carry that much blessing. The more you grow, the more you're blessed. I remember one time, I had been praying and believing for a specific amount of money that was required for my daughter's first year of college. Exactly three weeks before the money was needed, I got offered a project for the exact amount of money that I had been praying and believing for. I remember going on a walk that next morning and just praying and thanking God the whole time for coming through in such a miraculous way. Then God spoke to me, down in my heart, and said, "Imagine if you had added a zero to that figure? I'm only limited by what you believe I can do."

Well, I stopped dead in my tracks, right there in my subdivision, and lifted up my head to the heavens. It had never even come to mind to believe for more than that amount of money I had prayed for. I was under the impression that it was a huge amount of money at the time. And for me, it was. But, if you think in God's economy, it's just a trickle. He wants to bless us with so much. But, God can only bless us with what our lives and our beliefs can currently hold. He has to stretch us for more, and that's not always easy. I want you to believe for crazy blessing in your life. And I want you to live in such radical obedience, that blessing practically chases you down and overtakes you.

The first servant had done a great job. He was bold, obedient, and pressed through. He wasn't just getting a reward for it. He was getting the same kind of reward that his master enjoys—joy, delight, and blessedness. That's what God wants for you. The first servant got it. The second one did, too.

Then it was time for the last one to come forward. I can just see him now, dragging his feet, biting his lip, and trying to come up with some lame excuse as to why all he had in his hand was one bag of gold all covered in dirt. In desperation he came up with a doozie. He told the man that because he knew his master was a shrewd man and wouldn't want anything to happen to his money, he made sure he hid it really well! This sounds like an excuse to me. And an excuse is nothing more than a lie we create to protect us from a truth we're unwilling to accept. The excuse? He wanted to protect his master's money. The truth? He was scared and lazy. He then shows him that one lousy bag of gold and says, "See, here is what belongs to you" (v. 25). God didn't bless you so you could just flip it around and give it back to Him—untouched. He blesses us so we can use it, grow it, and expand it. That's what that whole "be fruitful and multiply" thing is all about!

That man didn't get to be a master of so much by being dumb, so he immediately saw through the malarkey. He responded to the third servant in no uncertain terms. He called him "wicked and lazy" and then said that the least he could have done would be to put the money in the bank where it could have accrued some interest. He then took the bag of gold from him and gave it to the first servant and threw the third servant out! He didn't mince words either. He said, "Throw that worthless servant outside, into the darkness, where there will be weeping and gnashing of teeth." Matthew 25:28

It was a pretty gutsy move for that first servant to take those five bags of gold and put them to work. He could have just invested two or three, but all five? Wow! That's bold! God loves boldness. It means we are acting in faith. Boldness can be operationally defined as "confidence that what you have to say or do is true and right and just." If we know what we are doing is right, then we can be bold in doing it. There is no fear, no reason for timidity. As a result of the first servant's boldness, he doubled his master's money! We need to be just as bold in the challenges that lie before us. There is no room for fear. You either act in boldness or you stand the risk of having your power taken away. If you already feel powerless, then you need to stand extra tall, hold those shoulders back, and step forward in faith like never before. You are in the position of power, no matter how much our culture tries to discredit who you are or what you can do! You have power and authority available to you through Jesus Christ and it's time to claim it!

In the story of the three servants, they were given bags of gold that were proportionate to their character. After spending time with all three, the master knew them inside and out. He gave the first one five bags because he knew that he was bold enough to invest it aggressively. To the second, he only gave two. I believe he was testing the waters with this guy. Perhaps he had proven himself with smaller tasks so he was letting him venture on to some greater responsibilities (and greater abundance). But that last guy…I think maybe the master was giving him one last shot. He had watched his servant being lazy and thoughtless. He had probably seen him make one dumb move after another, and cower in fear when opportunity rears its head. But he also saw something else. He saw a glimmer of hope, a shred of desire to create a better life than the one he was living. He knew, deep inside his servant, there were the skills and abilities to become extraordinary. That's probably why he hired him in the first place. He saw potential.

Character is a funny thing. Just when you think you know what someone is like, she's likely to up and surprise everybody. That last servant had a shot, and he totally blew it. Your character is not fixed. It is not something that is ingrained in us. It can change the moment you are willing to step over that line and say, "Enough!" Character is something that is proven. It is the way we face trials and overcome obstacles. It's that gold that begins to shine through in the perfecting process.

The first servant had proven his character and at the end of the story, he was left holding the bag (literally, the master gave him a bag of gold to keep). When God sees that we are acting in boldness and moving forward in faith, He will multiply our efforts and bless us abundantly. It must have been hard to double the money that had been entrusted to him, but the first servant persevered and sweated it out. Boldness is taking that vision that you have and acting on it with no turning back. It's hope in human form. You may be there right now, reaping the rewards of your diligence. You have acted on your power and authority and are seeing the blessings of God being manifested in your life. Keep standing firm! My challenge to you is to push beyond what you think is *possible*. God doesn't want to do something great through you. He wants to do something *impossible*.

The second servant proved himself as well. He didn't have as much as the first because the master probably knew that much responsibility would have totally freaked him out. God will meet us right where we are. That's not to say that He won't give us enormous responsibilities. He will. I guarantee. If He didn't, we would never be able to prove our character and push it to new levels. That second servant probably got two bags and thought, "Two bags? How in the world am I going to handle this enormous responsibility?" His heart was probably beating out of his chest and he had sweat dripping off his brow. But he did it. He stepped out in boldness and proved his position. The first servant probably acted the same way the first time he got two bags as well, and now there he stood with five!

God will continually put more and more responsibilities on us as he perfects us. I remember when I was pregnant with my second child. I called my mom crying because I didn't know how I was going to manage another baby when my first one took so much out of me. Now here I am with seven children! God will always provide ways to grow our character and improve our abilities, but we need to act in boldness and step forward in faith. You may be there right now, just realizing what power and strength you actually wield. You're sweating it out, but holding fast to the vision that God has given you for your life. You are being perfected in amazing—and challenging—ways. My challenge to you is to continue in faith. Act in boldness. And don't doubt in the darkness what God has revealed to you in the light.

That last servant stood a chance. He had it right there in his reach. He could have taken that bag of gold and worked his butt off to increase it. But, he probably thought there was no hope for him. "What can I possibly do with a bag of gold?" he probably thought to himself. "I can't even take care of myself. How can I take care of this gold?" Just the thought of the responsibility scared him so bad he went out and stuck it in the ground so he could just forget about it. He had a shot; and he blew it! If only he could have seen what the master saw in him— the hope, the potential. Just a little effort, that's all he needed to do, just to show his master that he was willing to give it a shot.

God just wants to see us try. He's not focused on your win at the finish line. He just wants to see you get up and run. The winning is God's job and He will find a way to do it through us—as long as we are taking action and acting in faith. You may

[Handwritten margin notes: - Parenting, - TZ, - K:change, - prayer, - inviting people to events.]

feel like that third servant. You just want to throw your hands up in hopelessness and say, "I give up." You have more power than you realize, and my challenge to you is to get up and give it a try. God sees the potential that lies within you. He would never give you the desire to live an abundant life if He did not intend on empowering you to accomplish it. <u>Whenever He authors something, He's more than able to finish it.</u> He just wants you to try. Yes, you may make mistakes and you may very well fall flat on your face. But the only real failure is when you choose not to get up and keep moving forward. <u>Even the mess-ups improve our abilities and mold our character.</u> <u>Don't run away from the responsibilities and don't ever think it's too late.</u> It's only too late if you fail to take the first step. God has handed you a bag of riches. What are you going to do with it?

The Law of Promotion

The parable of the talents is a perfect example of a universal law that God has set up since the beginning of time. It's called the Law of Promotion, and it's all summed up in one sentence that is right smack dab in the middle of what the master told the faithful servant in Matthew 26:21—*"You have been faithful and trustworthy over a little; I will put you in charge of much.* When God sees you being faithful in a little, He can promote you and put you in charge over much.

Fast cash is almost always followed by a fast crash. Have you ever noticed what happens when a pro athlete goes from a very modest salary to millions overnight? Usually within a year of their last touchdown, basket, pitch, or throw, they're broke or bankrupt. All of those millions passed right through their grasp because they did not have the skill, discipline, or faithfulness to handle it. A blessing can quickly become a curse if it lands on the wrong person. Look at the lottery—same story. You get a windfall and it knocks the wind right out of you!

How many of us would give our kid a brand spankin' new Harley a week after he took the training wheels off his bike? How many of us would hand the keys to a Mercedes to our kid after their first day in Drivers Ed? Hopefully, not many.

www.hannahhelpme.com

Blessings of that magnitude carry the potential to destroy a person. I was praying one morning, asking God why it was taking so long for my ministry to grow, and He answered me so distinctly. He said, "You wouldn't be able to handle it right now."

There is a reason God grows us slowly. It's because He wants us to persevere and handle the long haul. He doesn't want us to be his "child stars" that are thrust into blessing and then end up messed up and fizzled out. He's a gracious, loving God. He stretches us into abundance, slowly but surely.

That's how the Law of Promotion works. He gives us a little to grow our skills and abilities. When we master that, He gives us more. Seems easy enough, right? But this is one of the hardest principles for people to understand. Our human nature wants to take the easy way out. We want pills to lose weight instead of the self-discipline it takes to put down the fork. We want a loan to buy a car instead of taking the time to save up our money and buy it with cash. We want everything quick and easy—from buying a home to making macaroni and cheese. And herein lies the problem with abiding by the Law of Promotion.

I remember living in a cluttered home and convincing myself that if I had a bigger, nicer home, I wouldn't let it get cluttered. This is such deception! God will never give you bigger and better until you learn to handle smaller and lesser. What do you have right now? How are you handling it?

This is where that big "two-letter word" comes into play. IF we can show excellence with what we've been given, God will give us more. IF you want to be radically blessed, you need to start being radically obedient. God says to work as if you're working for God and not for man. How is that playing out in your home and with your career? Whatever you have right now is where you need to start sowing seeds of obedience.

Quit waiting for perfect to come along. There is no perfect! Perfection is a lie that keeps you paralyzed from making real progress. God wants you to be perfect-*ed*, not perfect. And this is a process. It means getting up every single day and choosing to give it your very best and refusing to fall for

My experience with my children is making me a better teacher & setting me up for work with TLC!

Crazy Mama

distraction or come up with any excuses. Your job is to be obedient. God's job is to bless. You can't do His job, and He won't do yours.

Deny Distraction

One of the biggest obstacles to obedience is that shiny, sparkly demon named "Distraction." A distracted person never wants to stay on task. They look for excuses to not do the work that lies before them. And in our culture of miniscule attention spans, we have to be entertained every moment of the day. If it's not fun, then forget it! I'm convinced that distraction kills. It is a tool used by the enemy to ruin our families, our homes, our businesses, and our dreams.

Distraction is one of the sneakiest and most effective tactics of the enemy to pull us away from productivity. Let's face it. We're all human; and the human tendency is to take the path of least resistance. If there's a shortcut, we'll use it. If there's an easy way out, we'll take it. Work is called "work" for a reason. It's rarely easy and it's almost always uncomfortable. But when it's done in the will of God, it's always, always, *always* fruitful. That's a big problem among a lot of people today—they confuse busy with fruitful. Being busy is work that doesn't yield anything positive. Being fruitful yields fruit. You've got something good to show for your efforts.

Distraction comes to us in a lot of forms, but it always pulls us away from obedience to what we should be doing. And it has never been easier to get distracted than in our current culture when we can't make it twenty minutes without glancing at our phone or computer. I firmly believe that the reason so many people seem to have an attention deficit is because our culture has created it, and we fall for it. We take the bait every time.

So what can you do? Well, denying distraction requires discipline; and discipline is never sparkly. In the words of Thomas Edison, "Opportunity is missed by most people because it comes dressed in overalls and looks like work. But, keep in mind that every time you fall for distraction, you are saying "yes" to the flesh and "no" to the spirit. It's the same battle that has been going on for centuries. Look at what Paul had to say about this struggle in his letter to the Galatians:

> "But I say, walk and live [habitually] in the [Holy] Spirit [responsive to and controlled and guided by the Spirit]; then you will certainly not gratify the cravings and desires of the flesh (of human nature without God). For the desires of the flesh are opposed to the [Holy] Spirit, and the [desires of the] Spirit are opposed to the flesh (godless human nature); for these are antagonistic to each other [continually withstanding and in conflict with each other], so that you are not free but are prevented from doing what you desire to do. (Galatians 5: 16,17)

Yes, we crave distraction. It's true. Obedience is hard. Work is hard; and our flesh is constantly looking for the way out. And it's not too hard to find. Paul didn't even have a Facebook account, and he still struggled. But, like he said, the spirit and the flesh are in constant opposition. The Spirit of God within us wants to get *results*. Our flesh wants *instant gratification.* And the two mix about as well as nacho cheese and marshmallows. In other words, they don't. The only result you get from instant gratification is prolonged destruction. *Distraction equals destruction.*

We know we should stay on task, but we badly want to steer away to something else. But we have the power to say "no" to the flesh. Oh, and I've got some bad news and good news for you. First, the bad news: It's going to be one of the most difficult things you do. It never gets easy. And now for the good news: Every time you choose to say no instead of yes, to stay instead of steer, *it gets easier.*

Paul said it perfectly, "walk and live [habitually] in the [Holy] Spirit." We have to make it a habit to stay on-task and not get distracted; and the habits that will yield the best results are almost always the hardest to create. Not impossible, but hard. And you can manage that. I know you can.

Discipline and obedience is like bodybuilding (minus the Creatine and the bronzing lotion). Every time you strain your muscle and lift a weight, you are actually tearing small fibers in the muscle tissue. The repair of that muscle tissue is what builds bulk and increases strength. Every time you deny that sparkly demon and push through with the task you have before you, you are tearing the flesh, breaking that distractive nature down so that the Holy Spirit can do the repair work and strengthen you to be more productive and fruitful with your life. You can ask any bodybuilder at the gym. When they first got started it was hard—really, *really hard*. But as they developed those habits of waking up each morning, going to the gym, and lifting, it got easier and easier. It never gets easy. It gets easi-*er*.

Anyone can start something. There's nothing special about that. When you start something new you are excited about it. You've got a vision about the way you want it to turn out and you're totally pumped. But as soon as the goosebumps die away, the monotony creeps in. And if you're like most people, you're ready to abandon ship.

The excitement and goosebumps can only keep you going for so long. It's exciting to think that you're going to get your finances under control and finally break out of debt, but after a lot of long months of scraping by and doing without, the coupon clipping gets boring and paying in cash at the grocery store becomes a dull chore. And when you think about how long it's going to take, you're just ready to call it quits and whip out the credit cards. It's like that with every challenge in our lives—getting in shape, keeping house, improving our business skills, working on our marriage—everything. And the one common denominator about success in all these areas is that it requires discipline.

I encourage you today to stick it out. You have everything in you to succeed on a level that you can probably not even imagine right now. But it's going to take diligence, discipline, and unwavering faith. God wants you to be blessed. I know that. You know that. The real question is, how bad do you want it?

The Blueprint to Blessing
Are you ready to be blessed like crazy? Now, you know the steps and now, you have the blueprint. God has a blood-bought covenant to bless you like crazy. But you have a responsibility to be obedient like crazy. Yes, people are going to think you're wacky. But that means that you're on the right path. When you choose to live like no one else, God is going to bless you beyond your wildest dreams.

It's your time to be blessed! I declare it right now, in the name of Jesus Christ and in the authority of God Almighty, you are blessed above all. You are blessed when you go out and when you come in. You are blessed to be the top and not the bottom. You were designed for blessing. God breathed it in you before the foundations of this earth were laid. It covers you. It goes before you. It hems you in from behind. When you step into a room, demons scatter and flee because the blessing of Almighty God goes with you! There is no challenge that can defeat you. There is no obstacle that can withstand your force. There is no weapon that is formed against you that can in any way, at any time, prosper. Abundance chases you down. Favor overwhelms you at every turn. You have chosen to live a life that is uncompromised. You have dedicated yourself to living in God's wisdom instead of man's. And because of your decision to stand out, to stand firm, and live like crazy, you will be blessed like crazy!

CRAZY BONUS!
Don't stop now. This is just the beginning, honey! Check out this FREE video, "The Three Secrets" to find out the three things you MUST do to reach success. Click on the link <u>RIGHT HERE</u>, or visit www.hannahkeeley.com/blog/3secrets

DID YOU ENJOY THIS BOOK?

Please let us know by leaving a review. Just <u>CLICK HERE</u> or visit the www.hannahlepme.com/crazy. Your review helps share the news that God wants to bless His children like CRAZY! Plus, if you leave a review, we'll send you a gift.

How's that for being a crazy mama?

Made in the USA
Charleston, SC
08 April 2016